PITS AND PITMEN
OF BARNSLEY

To Michael

PITS & PITMEN

of Barnsley

A pictorial tribute and celebration of miners, their families
and communities, 1900-2000

Best Wishes
Brian Elliott

BRIAN ELLIOTT

Wharncliffe Books

Dedication

For our children and grandchildren

First Published in 2001 by
Wharncliffe Books
an imprint of
Pen and Sword Books Limited,
47 Church Street, Barnsley,
South Yorkshire. S70 2AS

Copyright © Wharncliffe Books 2001

For up-to-date information on other titles produced under the
Wharncliffe imprint, please telephone or write to:

> **Wharncliffe Books**
> **FREEPOST**
> **47 Church Street**
> **Barnsley**
> **South Yorkshire S70 2BR**
> **Telephone (24 hours): 01226 - 734555**

ISBN: 1-903425-03-4

A CIP catalogue record of this book is available from the
British Library

Cover illustration: Front: A Barrow Colliery deputy making notes, 1951. *Harris Collection*
Back: Woolley miners return to work in 1985. *Ralph Summerfield*

Printed in the United Kingdom by
CPI UK

CONTENTS

A half-pulley wheel in commemoration of Grimethorpe Colliery. *Brian Elliott*

On the plaque:

COURAGE INITIATIVE DETERMINATION

THIS TABLET IS ERECTED TO COMMEMORATE
THE SERVICES OF J.A.HALL. PRESIDENT OF THE
YORKSHIRE MINEWORKERS ASSOCIATION
FOR HIS OUTSTANDING SKILL AND COURAGE
AT THE BARNBOROUGH DISASTER WHERE 13
OUT OF 17 LIVES WERE SAVED AND FOR HIS
UNCEASING EFFORTS TO SAVE LIFE AT MANY
OF THE MINING DISASTERS IN THIS COUNTRY
INCLUDING THE FOLLOWING · BULLCROFT
NORTH GAWBER · WHARNCLIFFE WOODMOOR
UPTON · BARNSLEY MAIN · CRIGGLESTONE
GRESFORD NORTH WALES.

1. 'Our Joe', Yorkshire Miners' leader Joseph Hall (see 79) is aptly
commemorated by this plaque that can be seen centre-stage in the
magnificent interior of the Miners' Hall of the Union Headquarters,
Huddersfield Road, Barnsley. *NUM*

INTRODUCTION

by Brian Elliott

This book is not intended as an academic history of mining in and around Barnsley. For those of us interested in industrial archaeology and technical aspects of coal mining, the book offers little interest. My aim has been to assemble and select pictures illustrating aspects of work and life of Barnsley miners and their families within the setting of the communities in which they lived, from about 1900 to the start of the millennium. Inevitably, editing has taken place and on occasions personal selection and availability of material has overriden historical perspective. But many of the 270 images that do appear are significant social documents.

In order to facilitate picture searching and selection I began by compiling a chronology of 'Barnsley coalfield events' but set within a regional and national framework, and I am grateful to Dave Douglass for checking my efforts, though any errors firmly remain my own. I was able to draw upon previously published pictorial works such as John Threlkeld's two-volume *Pits* books (1987-89), Robert G. Neville's, *The Yorkshire Miners in Camera* (1975), Anthony Burton's *The Miners* (1976) and Rosemary Preece's *Coal Mining and the Camera* (1998) as more than useful exemplars. I also have had the advantage of access to the excellent files of the *Barnsley Chronicle*, particularly for the post-1980 period. The generosity of former Grimethorpe miner Johnny Wood in allowing access to his vast collection of mining memorabilia has also been a great advantage, as has the kindness of Mel Dyke in sharing with me her collection of children's writings, photographs and precious material collected when she was deputy head at Willowgarth High School. Last but by no means least has been the immense contribution made by former miners and their families. Without their help this compilation would have been impossible.

One of the saddest days of my life was that Black Tuesday in October 1992 when the great pit closure announcement sent shock waves through our mining communities. And yet, like an expected bereavement, it had been forecast by the miners' union at least ten years earlier. The rector of Darfield, Martin Brown, described the Government's action as 'extraordinary and unbelievable' whilst Tony McPherson, vicar of Grimethorpe, referred to the 'shell-shocked' state of the miners, and the announcement as 'a shattering blow to an already hard-hit community'. In 1992 I was working at a further education college at Dinnington, in a community not unlike Grimethorpe. The college, built in 1928 as a mining and technical institute, was about to experience massive organizational and curriculum changes. The local pit had just closed and 'regeneration' was the buzz word of the new mission statement. The sense of personal loss and anger that I experienced was felt by many colleagues with family associations in mining communities. My father, who was born during the First World War, worked at Wharncliffe Woodmoor 1, 2 and 3 colliery, a young man when an explosion killed 58 men there in 1936. My uncles were miners and my aunts married miners. Grandfather Elliott worked underground at Dodworth and Monckton Main collieries, a hard working head of a family of ten who died relatively young. I have a Victorian studio photograph of my great grandfather, Jonas Elliott and his family, taken not long before he died, aged 47. He looked to be in his sixties or seventies, a victim of diseased lungs from dreadful working conditions in ganister and coal pits. His eldest son, George, followed his father's work, dying just four years later, aged 30. Many of us thought about our family histories back in 1992.

As part of the research for this book I was able to gain access to the archives at the National Union of Miners' headquarters in Barnsley. My heartfelt thanks go to Philip Thompson for facilitating this. It was also an opportunity to see part of the interior of this historic building. Anyone entering the Miners' Hall can not help but appreciate a strong sense of Barnsley and Yorkshire mining history in a most magnificent setting. Memorials to former miners' union leaders, a sculptured 'industrial' frieze, memorable cameos in stained glass, historic banners and a collection of mining artifacts and memorabilia all add interest and – with a little imagination – the voices of Joe Hall and Herbert Smith might be heard.

We are coming to the end of that generation of men and women who were born in coal mining communities in the early years of the twentieth century. Like Great War veterans, their voices speak to us across the years in a way that cannot be appreciated by sole reference to the written and printed word. It has been a great privilege and inspiration to know Arthur Clayton of Hoyland, local historian, former miner and friend who celebrates his one hundreth birthday in 2001. The importance of oral testimony remains crucial regarding those men and women of my father's age, at school during the 1926 strike and soon following their father's pitboots. In more recent times the closure and vindictive eradication from the landscape of all our collieries has made it even more important to safeguard and celebrate our family and community history – for the sake of future generations. Community interest in literary and artistic activity during and after the 1984-85 strike and the excellent work done in many of our local schools constantly shows us that our mining history has not and will not be forgotten. Through accidents and disasters, industrial disease and poverty, strikes and soup kitchens, marches and demonstrations, there are few industries with a stronger sense of the past.

2. Fred Massingham (1888-1971) who as a boy started work at Darfield Main in 1900. From 1912 until his retirement in 1953, Fred worked at Dearne Valley Colliery where he was a pit deputy and overman. He is seen here, in 1935, as leader of the Dearne Valley Rescue Team. *Colin Massingham*

ACKNOWLEDGEMENTS

I would like to gratefully acknowledge the assistance of the following individuals and organizations:

Allan Armstrong, Hazel Arnold, Debbie Allen, Barnsley Archives and Local Studies Library, *Barnsley Chronicle*, Elaine & David Biffen, Terry Bowman, Ivy Bradburn, Helen Brookes, Tony Capstick & BBC Radio Sheffield, Walter Caswell, Arthur Clayton, Dave Douglass, Mel Dyke, Jackie Garforth (Harris Collection), John Goodchild, Grimethorpe Miners' Welfare & Institute, Grimethorpe Regeneration Executive, G. Hall, Robert Harper (the late), Wes Hobson, Keith Hopkinson, Martin Jenkinson (professional photographer), Mel Jones, Ernest and Rita Kaye, The Labour Party, Mr and Mrs C. Lee, Lord Mason of Barnsley, Colin Massingham, Terry Middleton, National Mining Museum for England, National Union of Mineworkers, Ron Palmer, Mary Parry, Terence Picken, Grace Pollendine, Roy Portman, George Rawson, Jim Ritchie, Pauline Sapsford, Emma Sawyer (House of Commons Information Office), Chris and Pearl Sharp, Ralph and Maureen Summerfield, Ian Walker, Councillor Arthur Whittaker, Willowgarth High School, Yorkshire Arts Circus. All uncredited photographs are from the author's own collection.

Finally, my thanks go to Mike Parsons, Imprint Manager at Wharncliffe Books, Chief Executive Charles Hewitt and Pen and Sword's excellent production team.

3. Retired miner Colin Massingham (son of Fred Massingham), born Victoria Street, Darfield in 1925, shown here with pick and helmet but in smart attire, outside his home in Edward Street, Wombwell on 6 November 2000. Colin started work on the screens at Dearne Valley, aged fourteen in 1939, earning 18s 11d [95p] a week but after several other pit-top jobs was soon working underground as a 'gummer', keeping the Siskol coal-cutting machine clean of waste. Colin would wear a pair of hob-nailed boots, stockings, short-legged shorts and helmet, otherwise naked from the waist upwards. Lighting was via a heavy 2-volt CEAG electric handlamp, preferred by Dearne men to cap lamps. Colin worked briefly as a pony driver at Darfield Main (1946) but when Dearne Valley closed in 1967 he was employed on the pit top at Houghton Main as a timekeeper and fuel control officer, accepting voluntary redundancy in 1985.
Brian Elliott

Chapter One
1900-1920 : COAL TOWN

4. An Edwardian postcard or 'songcard', one of a series produced by Bamforth of Holmfirth on the theme of *Don't Go Down the Mine Dad*, a popular rendition of the day. Mining accidents and disasters had wrecked the lives of hundreds of Barnsley area families and devasted mining communities.

5. An assembly of miners on May Day Green, in about 1900. Outdoor meetings were called during times of dispute and for the annual 'Miners' Monday' holiday. There was a long tradition of organized and impromptu workers' gatherings in Barnsley.

6. A group of miners in typical pit clothes, believed to be at Higham on a summer's day c.1900. Several of the men are smoking from clay pipes and all but one wears a cap. Neckwear via tied handkerchief or scarf is evident as is clogs. Interestingly, lapel (union?) badges are visible on at least half of the men's jackets.

7. This c1912 image of a Nottinghamshire miner lying prone and 'hand-holing' or undercutting a coal seam supported by short sprags of timber, is from the camera of the well-known photographer Reverend Francis Cobb. *NCB*

8. The introduction of electric coal-cutting machines such as this Clarke and Steavenson example at the Lidget Colliery, near Hoyland Common, greatly increased output though operating the unguarded machine was a dangerous job still involving a lot of hard labour. *G.Beedon and B.Cocking*

9. Steel roof supports were introduced in some mines during the early 1800s. A couple of deputies and three lads hold still for the camera in this 1891 promotional lantern slide for Firths Patent Steel Props.

10. Here we have an unusual vertical view taken from the headgear looking down a shaft.

11. Two iron buckets or kibbles, used to lower men and materials during sinking operations are displayed. The smaller example is described as a 'mortar trunk' and the larger as a 'sinking trunk'. The term 'hoppet' was also used.

12. In the final example, two men are dwarfed by what appears to be the casing of a huge ventilation fan.

13. King George V arriving at Elsecar Main on Wednesday,10 July 1912. One old miner recalled to me, in December 2000, that as a boy he remembered the royal car passing through Hoyland on its way to Elsecar. *Old Barnsley*

14. The King, the Earl Fitzwilliam and other dignitaries emerging from the cage after spending forty minutes underground. The visit took place in the wake of the Cadeby Disaster when an explosion killed 35 men and a second blast took the lives of 53 rescuers, including three H.M. Inspectors of Mines. Many men had taken a shift off work to catch a glimpse of the royals visiting Conisbrough Castle, otherwise the scale of the tragedy would have increased four or five times.

15. This Edwardian postcard provides us with a good view of the new surface buildings at Elsecar Main alongside the railway and a canal basin, which as we can see was also used for swimming! Records examined by Mr A.K. Clayton tell us that two shafts were sunk between 1905-8, to the Parkgate seam at depths of 344 and 350 yards. *Old Barnsley*

16. Old Row, a terrace of fifteen workers' houses built at at Elsecar in the late eighteenth century. We know from census records that 98 people lived in the row from 1841-51, aged from 0.5 to 73.

17. Wentworth Woodhouse, the palatial mansion of one sometime resident family: the Fitzwilliams.

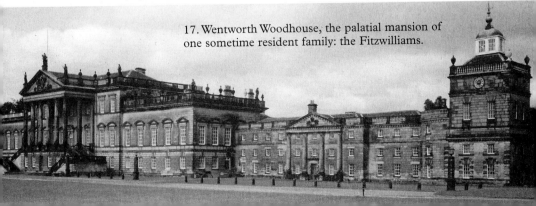

18. Benjamin Pickard (1842-1904) became an increasingly important figure in mining trade unionism. At the young age of 31 he was elected as Assistant Secretary to the West Yorkshire Miners' Association and rose to became the first Secretary of the new Yorkshire Miners' Association (which replaced the West Yorkshire and South Yorkshire associations). Pickard's popularity was reflected in his election as National President of the Miners' Federation of Great Britain in 1889. He was the first (of six) Yorkshire miners' leaders to serve as National President of the Union.

19. An early view of what the Edwardian postcard sender described as 'the colliers metropolis' or Yorkshire miners' headquarters on Huddersfield Road, Barnsley. At its opening in 1874 the Yorkshire Miners Secretary John Normansall contrasted the fine building with the dreadful working conditions, injuries and loss of life that mining communities had to endure.

MINERS' OFFICES, BARNSLEY.

The Colliers metropolis. a G.

20. John Wadsworth when an MP for the West Riding of Yorkshire (S.Hallamshire area), from a photograph by Warner Gothard of Barnsley. Born at Rotherham in 1850, Wadsworth started work as a pit lad and was employed at Newton Chamber's Thorncliffe pit until the lockout of 1869. He worked at Wombwell Main during the Thorncliffe dispute, moving on to Wharncliffe Silkstone Colliery at Tankersley where in 1883 he was chosen by the miners as their checkweighman. His Yorkshire union interests continued, serving in various capacities until being elected President in 1904. It was said that he '[knew] what he wants to say in a speech, and says it in a very convincing manner, and is one of the most popular of the elected Miners representatives.' The image below is a specimen certificate given by the Wadsworths to election supporters. *NUM*

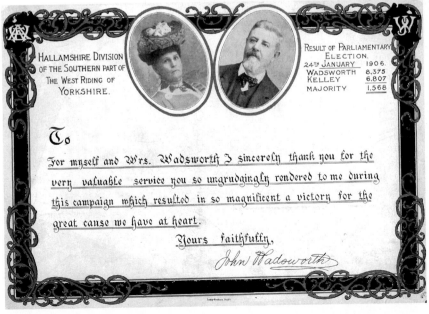

HALLAMSHIRE DIVISION OF THE SOUTHERN PART OF THE WEST RIDING OF YORKSHIRE.

RESULT OF PARLIAMENTARY ELECTION.
24TH JANUARY 1906.
WADSWORTH 8,375
KELLEY 6,807
MAJORITY 1,568

To

For myself and Mrs. Wadsworth I sincerely thank you for the very valuable service you so ungrudgingly rendered to me during this campaign which resulted in so magnificent a victory for the great cause we have at heart.

Yours faithfully,

John Wadsworth

21. Children of a miner: the Claytons of Hoyland Common, c.1903. *Left to right:* Friend (b.1898), who went on to work at Wharncliffe Silkstone (at Pilley), Hoyland Silkstone (Platts Common) and Rockingham, becoming an NCB inspector; Fred (b.1894), who worked at Hoyland Silkstone, Cortonwood and Rockingham, a union man; Arthur (b.1901) who started work at Hoyland Silkstone as a boy, then moved to Rockingham; Annie (b.1902) and Wilfred (b.1891) who worked at Rockingham, Cortonwood and Warsop Main. 'Pattie' who died aged seven was added on the right of the photograph. *A.K.Clayton*

22. A rare photograph (c.1890) of the pit yard at Carlton on Lord Wharncliffe's estate, believed to be on the occasion of a presentation of a sextant to the company (Wharncliffe Woodmoor Colliery Co Ltd) owner's son, E.A. Allport. *Mary Parry*

23. Evan Parry (1846-1912), his wife Ann (1847-1914) and their seven children. Evan had moved to Carlton from Mostyn (where the local pit had flooded) in North Wales, becoming a manager at Wharncliffe Woodmoor Colliery in 1884. Mel Jones has shown that Evan was a key figure in the establishment of a Welsh community in Carlton. *Mary Parry*

24. The Welsh Chapel at Carlton was demolished in 1984. The corrigated building which had cost just £200 had served the original migrants and their descendants since 1902. 'Tin Tabernacles' were a quick, convenient (they could be ordered from ironmasters' catalogues) and cheap place solution to communal worship in burgeoning mining communities. *Mel Jones*

25. On 6 May 1906 young miner Harry Sherburn (of Sheffield Road), his wife Clara and their two children boarded RMS *Coronia* at Liverpool, arriving in New York ten days later. A further two day's travel by sail and rail saw them arriving late on a Saturday evening at Matewan where Harry was to gain employment at the Red Jacket mine of the Matewan Mining Company. Thankfully, the Sherburn's great adventure (they returned to England on the *Lusitania* over two years later) was researched by Terry Bowman who has followed his great grandparents' footsteps. Harry and Clara are shown here on the right of this later studio photograph, with children Mary Grace and Edward. *Terry Bowman*

26 and 27. Clara and Harry (seated, centre) with children Mary Grace and Edward on the veranda of their new (mining company) home at Matewan;and a modern (1995) view of the same property, showing that there were few changes in the intervening years. *Terry Bowman*

DISASTER AT BARROW COLLIERY NEAR BARNSLEY. 15 NOV 1907.
SEVEN MEN (PHOTOGRAPHS ABOVE) WERE THROWN OUT OF CAGE AND INSTANTLY KILLED, FALLING A DEPTH OF 200 F.
THE OTHER NINE OCCUPANTS WERE MORE OR LESS SERIOUSLY INJURED.

28. While the Sherburns were in America news of the terrible cage disaster at Barrow Colliery, Worsbrough may well have reached them.

Seven young men (aged 18-35) were flung from an ascending double-deck open-fronted cage 200 feet to the bottom of the shaft at four in the afternoon on Friday 15 November 1907. A survivor, George Hargreaves gave a 'thrilling account' to the *Barnsley Chronicle*, describing how a footplate may have been left in place at a landing, causing the cage to suddenly tilt on its ascent, six men being thrown out of the top deck (where he grimly held fast) and one from the lower. He described the 45 minutes or 'fearful time' that the survivors, some badly injured, had to endure :

we dare not move, for we did not know what was coming next, and all we could sometimes hear was the groaning of men on the cage.

Typically, there were tragic scenes at the pit head in the aftermath of the disaster, as described in the same news report:

One young miner came to the cabin where the bodies were placed and asked to see one of them. The face was uncovered [and] throwing himself on his knees, he kissed the dead face and burst into tears. The corpse was that of his mate. The two had been working together in the afternoon.

This commemorative postcard was produced by Warner Gothard of Barnsley.

29. The old colliery rescue station at Tankersley. Erected in 1902, it was the first purpose-built station in the country, serving local collieries such as Rockingham, Wharncliffe Silkstone and Hoyland Silkstone. Another early (and well-equipped) station was built at Wath in 1908, Houghton Main included in its catchment area.

30. Probably the earliest surviving photograph of Grimethorpe Colliery first aid team, winners of the prestigious Wood Shield in 1911. They are (Left to Right): Dr Thompson, J. Rogerson, G. Pickles, P. Haley, S. Roebuck and T. Ryder and colliery manager S. Gill. *Ian Walker*

31 and 32. On Sunday 23 November 1907 sixty-one year old Francis ('Frank') Chandler of Jump village, a deputy at Hoyland Silkstone Colliery, was responsible for a gang of men occupied with underground repair work in the distant Parkgate seam when an 'earth bump' resulted in a girder, along with a considerable amount debris crashing onto the boilerhouse, penetrating the boiler and causing a sudden escape of steam. Frank, though badly scalded, carried one man to safety, checked on others and managed to crawl his way in total darkness, to the pit bottom, where he gained access to the cage and was eventually able to summon assistance. Unfortunately, one man (Arthur Greenwood) had been killed almost instantly and two others (Arthur Cooke and Leonard Chandler - aged just 19, Frank's son - died later). Apart from Frank, his other son, Lawrence and son-in-law, Isaac Scawthorpe were injured, along with Walter Sistern.

His heroism was praised at the inquest and Frank became the first recipient of the Edward Medal, awarded for bravery in coal mines. Although Frank Chandler died in 1924 (aged 86) there are still some memories of him proundly wearing his medal whilst walking the streets of Hoyland. A national hero, Frank travelled to London on 27 February 1908 and was greeted by a crowd of well-wishers at the Home Office before being conveyed to Buckingham Palace for the medal award ceremony.

The bearded hero looked almost identical to the King in this painting of the occasion, reproduced in the *Illustrated London News*. The other recipient was Henry Everson, a Glamorganshire miner. *NUM/Barnsley Archives and Local Studies*

33. Hoyland Silkstone Colliery, Platts Common, in about 1908. *Old Barnsley*

34 and 35. Pit rescue teams became an essential requirement for all collieries following the *Coal Mines Act* of 1911 and numerous photographs survive showing men (trained volunteers) and equipment. This interesting early team is from an unknown Barnsley area colliery, the rescue men wearing their oxygen masks in the lower picture. Despite increasing technology, the canary's sensitivity to gas meant that they continued to be a valued piece of safety 'equipment' for many years to come. *Old Barnsley*

36. Matron and nurses at Barnsley's Beckett Hospital. The original (1865) dispensary for outpatients was later extended to deal with the huge increase in coal mining injuries and was financed from endowments, subscriptions and from miners and coal owners of the area. *Old Barnsley*

37. Well before the introduction of the National Health Service, 'Hospital Sundays' were a popular way to raise money for charitable purposes, when church and chapel banners, hymn-singing and brass and comic bands took place alongside fancy dress exploits and performances from comic bands – as can be seen in this wonderful example, assembled ouside Dodworth Working Men's Club. *Old Barnsley*

38-40. Three further examples of montage postcards from the expanding studios of Warner Gothard. Cards were produced by this enterprising Barnsley-based business within a day or so of the occurrence of pit and other disasters – nationwide. Portraits from family albums were borrowed from widows and relatives in order to hurriedly produce a commemorative card which of course had considerable commercial potential, perhaps with a small amount of remuneration given to bereaved families.

The fourth example (41) is a compilation by Gothard of a tram accident at Bournemouth in 1908 which resulted in the loss of seven lives.

42. One of two photographs taken at 'Jagger's Pit' or Darton Main in celebration of reaching the Parkgate seam on 11 August 1914. Two of the men in the kibble are believed to be Mr Jagger, the mine owner and Mr Stone, a mines inspector. Pit sinkers, in their distinctive oilskins contrast with   suited men standing in the foreground. *Old Barnsley*

43. (Right) The second image, though of poor quality, shows a far larger assembly of men with a wheel barrow of extracted coal below the kibble. Some of the workers were recruited from Denby Dale and Skelmanthorpe, known as 'Yar-sarders' due to their strong accents.

44. As can be seen from this postcard produced by George Washington Irving, a serious fire caused widespread damage to surface buildings at Church Lane (Dodworth) Colliery in April 1907. Interestingly, the card was sent from Barnsley to Edward Sherburn of Matewan, West Virginia from 'Grandma' on 8 May (see 25-27). My paternal grandfather worked at Dodworth pit about this time. *Terry Bowman*

45. Walter Caswell (b.10 December 1915, Carlton). Like many other pit lads, Walter's first job was on the screens, sorting the coal from the dirt. He was just under the age of fourteen when he commenced work at Wharncliffe Woodmoor 1, 2 and 3 colliery in 1929. It was a dirty, dusty and very noisy workplace, the gaffer having to shout and bawl instructions and reprimands. In winter a fire was kept at each end of the open building, the boys warming by it whenever there was a pause in operations. This was also a good place to place his bottle of tea. After a seven and a half hour shift he often worked a further three hours carrying pit props which were being made ready to go underground the next day. *Brian Elliott*

46. A pause in operations at the Barnsley Main screens. Two of the lads look much younger than thirteen in this compelling Edwardian photograph. Older men and those not fit enough to work underground were also employed on screen work. Combined with oral testimony, such views are of considerable interest to anyone researching the social history of mining. *Old Barnsley*

47. This photograph of the screens at St Hilda Colliery, South Shields, dating from 1901, suggests a military style operation. Notice the foreman with his long stick! One old Barnsley miner (b.1901) told me how the screen gaffer used to shout the following endearing words to any day dreaming lad: 'I'll cut your liver out and put it back and swear I never touched you.'

Ada Walshaw

Herbert Walshaw

Lewis Walshaw

Flory Walshaw

48. 'Cuckoo Pit', Whin Moor, rear of Noblethorpe Hall. A group of Silkstone miners and their families digging for coal during the 1912 strike. The dispute - largely on the issue of a minimum wage - just about closed every pit in Britain. After many weeks of hardship the Miners' Federation had to weigh up an acceptance of the Government's hurriedly assembled Act which ensured minimum rates of pay for face workers but had to be agreed at district rather than national level. *Old Barnsley/Jim Ritchie*

49. The smaller photograph shows striking miners digging for coal in 1912 at Warren Quarry Lane, a few minutes walk from the centre of town, an area where outcropping had probably taken place from medieval times. The postcard was inscribed with a tongue in cheek 'Don't Go Down the Mine Daddy' caption. At many schools in Barnsley breakfasts were provided by the Salvation Army for the children of striking miners.

Mrs Graham

Mrs Dawson

Ambrose Holmes or
Mash Holmes

Vulmer Hasty

Tom Mann

Daff Garnet or
Ambrose Padget

MINERS MEET AT BARNSLEY

STIRRING SPEECHES

SIMULTANEOUSLY with the Wombwell gathering, a meeting was held in the Arcadian Hall, Wellington Street, Barnsley, at which several speakers referred to the minimum wage question. Miners were present from the Barrow, Barnsley Main, Monk Bretton, Wharncliffe Woodmoor, Kendall Green, Round Green, Strafford Main, Strafford Rob Royd, Central Silkstone, Woolley, Stanhope Silkstone, North Gawber, Darton, Primrose Main, Harbro' Hills, Old Silkstone, Church Lane, Carlton Main collieries. The hall was crowded to its utmost capacity, and many were unable to find admittance.

Mr. Thos. Phipps, of Strafford, presided, supported by Mr. John Dixon (financial secretary of the Yorkshire Miners' Association), Mr. Thomas Duerden (Carlton Main), Mr. Thorne (Church Lane), and others.

The Chairman said it was encouraging to find the miners of the Barnsley district so interested in this very important question. They were determined that the question of a minimum wage should be settled one way or another, and that before long. (Applause.)

Mr. Duerden said the workers of Yorkshire would not rest satisfied until a minimum wage was obtained for the miners right throughout the Kingdom. (Applause.) It was high time the great Federation that had been booming during all these years, did something for its members. (Applause.) The day when this question was to be brought to a head had been a long time coming, but he hoped that the workers would now stick loyally together, and see to it that their efforts were crowned with success. (Hear, hear.) There ought to be a minimum rate of wages for all workers in the mine — boys as well as men — (applause). The honest working boy, who did his best from week-end to week-end, should know that he was to have a fixed sum to draw every pay day, and when he reached a certain age he should, provided that he was a skilled worker be entitled to a certain minimum wage. (Hear, hear.) Mr. Duerden complained that under the present system there was no protection whatever for by-workmen, who could be set on at whatever work the management had a mind. ("Shame.") These men should have a fixed rate as well as anyone else. (Hear, hear.)

"If the Federation had taken this question up at the colliery where I worked Carlton Main would not be in the position to-day that it is in," declared Mr. Duerden warmly. A man who was willing to work, left his house, and went to work, should be assured of a day's wage, notwithstanding that for some reason or other he was unable to do all of his work for that day. (Hear, hear.) People asked where was the money going to come from? Where had it come from up to this? It had come out of the workers. They had been the sufferers all through, but they really believed that many difficulties would be removed if a fixed minimum standard wage all round were fixed (Applause). They were told that the great difficulty in regard to the fixing of a minimum wage was on account of the old men. That sort of talk was pure bluff. (Hear, hear.) Having expressed the hope that the meeting would be unanimous in favour of a minimum wage, Mr. Duerden moved the following resolution :—

That this meeting, after hearing the reports of the Miners' Federation on the minimum wage question, resolves to support our leaders to obtain a minimum wage for workers in the mine. (Hear, hear.)

50. The 'minimum wage question' was the subject of a packed meeting of miners held at the Arcadian Hall, Wellington Street in 1912 under the chairmanship of Thomas Phipps of Strafford Collieries. *NUM*

51. A postcard by A. Eagle of Barnsley reflecting one of the most popular of miners' interests: allotment gardening and keeping pigeons. The family appear to be in their Sunday best for the occasion. *Old Barnsley*

52. For many young miners, playing for the village or colliery football team was a passionate but pleasant change from the pit; and yet they were competing with and usually against fellow miners. Here we can see the Darton and Woolley Colliery team during season 1910-11. *Old Barnsley*

53 & 54. A rare and interesting photograph of Strafford Rob Royd Colliery in about 1910. We have a good view of some of the key surface buildings: the wooden headstock, cage and pulley wheels, cupola chimney and steam-powered engine house but what makes the composition particularly interesting is the parade of men and horses (not ponies, used for pulling tubs) in the foreground. By his dignified appearance, the man on the right may have been someone of authority. In later years the pit was used as an air and man-riding shaft belonging to the Strafford Colliery Company (of Stainborough) and, as can be seen by the photograph of 1977, some of the old stone buildings of the pit could still be glimpsed at the side of the M1 motorway. *Old Barnsley & A.K.Clayton*

Two period advertisements remind us that in the years preceding the Great War, Coal was King.

55. A 1909 advert for M. Lowrance & Son's patent 'Trident Kitchen' ranges; and

56. Mark Oldham's 'All Descriptions of Coal on Hand' (1914).

Chapter Two
1921-1940 : DISTRESS AND POVERTY

57. Ernest and Mildred Kaye in their Burton Road home, November 2000.

Born in 1917, Ernest started work as a door trapper at Rockingham Colliery, aged fourteen where his father, Albert, had once worked. As a schoolboy Ernest remembers sinking a pit in allotments during the 1926 strike. It was worked via a bicycle wheel, rope and bucket, and a candle for light. Each man was allowed two buckets of coal. Birdwell WMC gave free teas (two jam sandwiches and a bun) to children. He also recalled the family having few clothes and coal-picking on the muck stack at Pilley, filling a sack which was taken home via the frame of his bicycle to his Birdwell home for his father to empty and make ready for a return trip. Timber for making fires were also obtained from Rockley Wood. After several years working underground at Rockingham, Ernest moved on to Wharncliffe Silkstone at Pilley, then Houghton Main where he retired after 47 years in mining.

58. Ernest Kaye as a boy.

Labour Party Library

YESTERDAY - THE TRENCHES

59 & 60. After the Great War there was a general feeling that the men who had been sent to the trenches did not receive their just rewards on returning to civilian life. The spectre of mass unemployment beckoned, according to these Labour Party posters.

TO-DAY—UNEMPLOYED

61. A miner's wife on a routine visit to the pawnshop. Miners were hard hit by the slump, suffering from low wages and – in many pits – dreadful working conditions.

62. The impressive façade of Horsfields, Sheffield Road, one of Barnsley's best known pawnbrokers. It was a very busy shop during the 1920s. From flat irons to best suits and 'family jewels', in fact anything of value was exchanged at the discrete pledging office at the side of the premises.

63. Soup kitchens were established at many locations in and around the Barnsley area during the 1921 and 1926 miners' strike. This one, by the Barnsley Salvation Army, served 300-500 free dinners daily in 1921.

64. A superb atmospheric photograph showing the pit deputies of the Wharncliffe Woodmoor 1, 2 and 3 rescue team, wearing 'Proto' breathing apparatus, dating from the 1920s. They are (Left to Right): Mr Parkinson (instructor/leader), Walter Trimby, William Turton, Jack Elrin and Sam Dutton. This was not the usual 'publicity' image that we often see, in fact the men had just emerged from the pit after dealing with an underground fire. Walter Trimby was killed in the pit shortly afterwards. *Mrs M. Goddard*

65. The Dearne Valley Colliery Rescue Team, with Rescue Car and station (probably at Barnsley Main) in the background, dating from 1935. They are (Left to Right) back row: T. Fisher, Jack Lockwood, Tom Marsh, J. Parkinson (instructor), Maurice Bray and John ('Long John') Worthington (pit manager); front row (Left to Right): Fred Massingham and Jack Welford. *Colin Massingham.*

66. A typical advertisement for the 'Proto' breathing apparatus and other safety equipment used by rescue teams, made by Siebe, Gorman and Co. Ltd of Lambeth, London. *From W.E. Skinner's Mining Year Book for 1930.*

The
WOOTTON
SAFETY LANTERN
•

THE WOOTTON SAFETY LANTERN has been passed by the Mines Department and included in the Safety Lamps Order under Section 13 of the Coal Mines Act, 1911.

With this Lantern, objects at a distance of 100 to 150 yards can easily be examined, whilst at the same time, for general inspection work, a different light may be obtained by merely rotating the bezel through an angle of forty-five degrees.

Lead seals are supplied so that the Lantern may be effectively sealed, thus preventing unauthorised persons from tampering with it.

PRICES :

Type C.956. Complete with Accumulator and Bulb - £2 6 6

Type C.956M. Complete with Indicating Accumulator, which at all times clearly indicates the state of charge, also Bulb at - - - £2 7 9

Special Terms Quoted for Collieries, etc.

Write for Catalogue.

S. SMITH & SONS (Motor Accessories) Ltd., Cricklewood, LONDON, N.W.2.

68. The 'Wootton' safety lantern was manufactured by Smiths of Cricklewood, London. From a 1930 advertisement.

Note the reference to the 1911 *Coal Mines Act.*

67. An even more detailed 1930 advert under the 'Everything for Safety Everywhere' slogan adopted by Siebe Gorman.

"Everything for Safety Everywhere."

"PROTO" BREATHING APPARATUS

For rescue and recovery work in mines after explosions, etc.

SMOKE HELMETS

OXYGEN RESUSCITATING APPARATUS

GAS MASKS

GAS ANALYSIS APPARATUS

AND ALL OTHER

SAFETY AND PROTECTIVE APPLIANCES

SIEBE, GORMAN & CO., LTD.,

"NEPTUNE" WORKS, 187, WESTMINSTER BRIDGE ROAD, LAMBETH, LONDON, S.E.1.

Telegrams: "Siebe, Lamb, London." Telephone: Hop No. 3401 (2 lines).

69. Pit pony races were held at Darfied during the 1921 strike. Here, Tom Pantry, horse-keeper at Dearne Valley Colliery, shows off *Doctor*, the winner of the pit pony derby. Other events included the 'Snape Hill Stakes', 'Highfield Handicap', 'Low Valley Selling Plate' and 'Darfield St Leger'. *W.T.Hollins*

70. Repairing a Main Roadway, from a 1930s painting by Vincent Evans.

71 & 72. A.J. (Arthur James) Cook, the Welsh miners' leader (b. Wookey, Somerset, 1883) came to national prominance during the 1926 strike when Secretary of the Miners' Federation. Cook was imprisoned in 1918 and 1921 for his leadership of striking miners.

An inspirational speaker, he was a passionate advocate and agitator, constantly 'fighting' the low wage/long hours demands of the mine owners. Mr Arthur Clayton (b.1901), a former Rockingham miner recently told me that, along with several other men from Hoyland, he walked to Thorpe Hesley to hear Cook speak during the 1926 dispute. He was then at the height of his fame as a speaker and Arthur recalls that Cook's voice seemed hoarse as though it had been overstrained, a consequence of a busy schedule of public meetings. There was an ironic moment when the sound of clogs could be heard clattering outside the large army hut in which a large crowd had assembled. 'Look through t'window Cookie', shouted the colliers. Miners from a nearby pit – still working– were walking home. Cook made a casual remark and resumed his speech. The strike was nearing its end. Arthur also recalled hearing Cook addressing a crowd from the balcony of Tankersley Welfare Hall one Sunday evening. A.J.Cook died in London, in 1931, aged only 48.

73. A compelling photograph of Jump village 'Distress Committe' sums up the suffering experienced by many miners' families during the 1926 strike – and typifies the self-help approach of small mining communities.

74. Popular Yorkshire miners' leader Herbert Smith (b.1862). Born in the workhouse and a pit boy at the age of ten, Smith was President of the Yorkshire Miners Association from 1906 until his death in 1938, so was a very familiar figure in Barnsley. John Threlkeld described his appearance as 'sporting a flat cap the size of a large dustbin lid and [wearing] an English lever watch the size of a small dustbin lid', one of his most memorable phrases, 'Now't doin' apparently used in defiant response to Baldwin's proposal to increase miners' hours and cut pay. There are many anecdotes concerning Herbert's honest and outspoken views of injustices and in particular his forthright reaction to colliery owners and politicians. One miner, who had heard Smith talk at Hoyland Common WMC, recalled how he had told the assembled crowd of a recent anticipated meeting with Baldwin: 'The Prime Minister has come, gentlemen' was the announcement. Herbert responded with 'I know that, I can smell him'. Smith never hesitated to take the mickey out of politicians with 'a ponderous kind of wit'. Herbert Smith died at his desk in a ground floor room of the Yorkshire Miners' Offices, Barnsley, in 1938.

Dear Sir,

re J. Butler.
- - - - - -

I have your letter of the 25th instant, and I am
sorry at receiving such a letter from you, as I know from
past experience that you try to do what you think is right,
but if I attempted to argue this case from a legal point of
view probably you would ask me to quote the Section in the
Workmens' Compensation Act, but I am not doing that; I
am dealing with this case as I should naturally expect to
deal with any other case, namely, this man has been disabled
from following his employment by working for your Company
at the Barmbro' Main Colliery - unfortunately for both
sides - but I think you will agree more unfortunate for
the workman from a living point of view. I have yet to
learn that you desire to be behind other Collieries in showing
your good-will towards men or boys who are in unfortunate
positions as the above-named, but I am not wishful to quote
other Collieries although I could quote many, and I always
thought that the Collieries under your supervision would be
in line with the most-advanced, but if your letter must be
taken in the way it is written I am afraid one has been
giving too much credit. This I am not prepared to say

[handwritten margin note: fact is, want except the 5/- the same as other light work]

75. A letter from Herbert
Smith to A.T. Thomson,
manager and director at
Manvers Main Collieries
Ltd, dated 26 July 1924.

Typically, Smith writes
in support of an injured
Barnburgh miner and his
dependents who had been
refused 'home coal',
suggesting to Thomson
that 'estranged
relationships' might ensue
between the
correspondents unless a
settlement was agreed.
Johnny Wood

has been done up to the present, and I again ask you
to kindly look into this matter from the humane point of view
and in justice to the injured workman and his dependents.
If you cannot settle kindly give me a few dates to select
from when you could meet so that you and I could talk
together on this question, as we ought to do nothing at any
time that will cause estranged relationships between us,
particularly if it can be done for the good of both, and
I suggest this would be so, so that this man is properly
cared for and kept comfortably at home, and be fit for work
sooner.

I may say that I have attended scores of
Collieries where men have been on compensation, and have
never yet been refused at one for the Company to supply
the man or men when on compensation with Home Coal.

Thanking you for a favourable reply.

Yours faithfully,

Hubert Smith

President.

A.T.THOMSON ESQR.,
Manvers Main Clls, Ltd,
Wath-upon-Dearne,
ROTHERHAM.

76. Herbert Smith addressing what may have been a meeting of area miners' leaders, possibly during the 1926 dispute. The are (Left to Right), standing: Herbert Smith, W.P. Richardson, F. Varley, Alf Smith, T. Straker, G. Annable, W. Smith (Leicester) and seated (Left to Right): T. Richards, N. Abblett, A.J. Cooke, Frank Hall, Sam Finney and S. Whitehouse. Smith was President of the Miners' Federation of Great Britain (1922-29) and International Miners Federation (1921-29). *NUM Archives*

Yorkshire Mine Workers' Association.

(ESTABLISHED 1858.   AMALGAMATED 1885).

7075.

MINERS' OFFICES,

BARNSLEY,

Decr. 8th.   1927

President: HERBERT SMITH.
Vice-President: ED. BOUGH.
Agent: ALF. SMITH.
Financial Secretary: J. A. HALL.
General and Corresponding Secretary: JOSEPH JONES.

Dear Sir,

We have to approach you with regard to No.9's
Stall in which the gross earnings due to the men were
paid to a man named Harris who absconded.   You
will be familiar with the past Judgements in cases of
this kind, and appreciate that the responsibility
of paying wages direct to the workmen concerned rests
upon the Employer.   We are informed that
you have undertaken to be responsible for half the
amount, and would thank you for a letter, after
reconsidering the matter, undertaking to assume the
responsibility for the remainder.   Afterwards it
would then be for the Employer to take steps to
issue a warrant for the apprehension of the person who
has absconded.

Your early and personal attention will oblige.

T. L. SOAR ESQ.,   Yours truly,
BARNBRO' MAIN COLLIERY.   GEN: SECY.
NR. DONCASTER.

77 & 78. A letter dated 8 December 1927, from Yorkshire Miners' General Secretary Joseph Jones to T.L. Soar of Barnbrough Main Colliery concerning an 'absconded' miner who appears to have disappeared with the gross payments of men working in 'No.9 Stall'. Note the circular image of the Miners' Offices, now shown on the letterhead. Jones became General Secretary three years earlier and during the '26' strike headed a fund raising delegation to America. He was to become National President of the Union in 1933 but after taking a lucrative position with the new Coal Commission in 1938 resigned from the National and Yorkshire Presidency. Understandably, the Union had protested at the prospect of Jones functioning in a dual working capacity, especially since the Commission's remit was to consider colliery amalgamations, concentrating production at 'economic pits'.

79. The successor to Herbert Smith was one of the most charismatic of all Yorkshire miners' leaders: Joseph 'Joe' Hall. A brilliant speaker, Joe, born at Lundhill, near Wombwell in 1887 and working at Darfield Main by the age of twelve, went on to earn the great respect of miners in Yorkshire and other coalfields by his supportive actions at mining disasters and during disputes. He retired in 1952. *NUM*

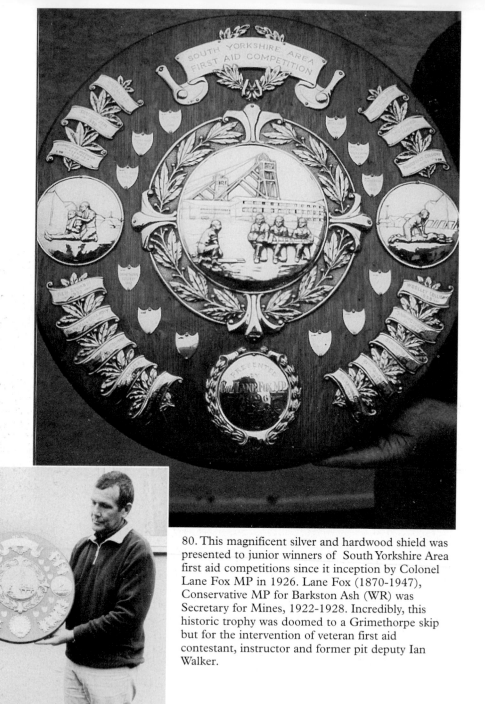

80. This magnificent silver and hardwood shield was presented to junior winners of South Yorkshire Area first aid competitions since it inception by Colonel Lane Fox MP in 1926. Lane Fox (1870-1947), Conservative MP for Barkston Ash (WR) was Secretary for Mines, 1922-1928. Incredibly, this historic trophy was doomed to a Grimethorpe skip but for the intervention of veteran first aid contestant, instructor and former pit deputy Ian Walker.

81. Ian Walker displays the 'Fox Shield' outside the St John's Ambulance building at Grimethorpe, November 2000. This extension block was built using donations from the Children in Need Appeal and opened in 1990 by Mrs Norah Waring, widow of Fred Waring BEM, founder member of the St John's Ambulance Brigade in Grimethorpe.

82. Wharncliffe Woodmoor 4 and 5 Colliery First Year Ambulance Team who won the prestigious Lane Fox Shield at Heckmondike in 1930. They are (Left to Right): William Wright, James Kershaw, Walter Caswell (instructor), Danny Carter and Harry Baker. Accompanying Walter Caswell was his young son, also called Walter (see image number 45) who acted as a 'patient' for the competition.

Walter Caswell senior was often called into action to attend to injured miners and his exceptional knowledge and skills were called upon six years later at the dreadful disaster at the neighbouring 1, 2 and 3 colliery.

Walter Caswell junior, now 85, told me that first aid classes were held at the Working Men's Club at the end of 'Long Row' (Carlton Terrace), Carlton. It was from these meetings that teams were entered for competitions.

83. It made sense for all concerned that well-trained men – usually fellow miners – were on hand to deal with injuries since accidents were such a regular part of working life.

First aid competitions were an incentive to test skills and knowledge and success in a prestigious competition brought both pride and recognition to pit teams, also providing a focus for further training. Barnsley Main ambulance team are seen here in this c1930 photograph with the Townsend Cup and individual trophies.

Left to right, back row: Stan Wortley, Herbert Townsend and Stan (?); front: Jack Hold (senior, team captain) and Jabez Crossland. *J. Roberts & Co*

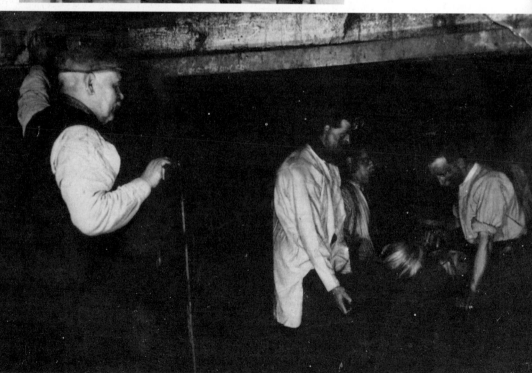

84. Realistic first aid practice also took place underground as can be seen in this example, taken at Hickleton Main in about 1925. The watching deputy is believed to be a Mr Bateman.

85. Young miners enjoying an open-air swim at Darfield Clay Hole during the hot summer of 1926. A superb social document of the time from the camera of Joe Short of Wombwell.

One former miner who was then in his mid-twenties, recalled many striking miners flocking to Elsecar reservoir, including some older men who learnt to swim for the first time. For some young miners the long strike provided opportunity for long walks in the countryside, for example from Hoyland into Derbyshire, returning on the train. Miners used to light a fire, make a sort of bivouac and cook meals in the open.

Holidays were of course rare events, so the fresh air and exercise would certainly have meant improved health, and possibly extended the life expectancy of many. Men lived on their savings, supplemented with a little money from the union. Every three weeks or so at Hoyland the bellman would walk around the streets announcing that there was, say five shillings (25p), to be collected at the weekend; and a communal kitchen for children was provided at the working men's club. Payment took place in the mornings, often followed with a band concert. *R.J. Short*

86. Royston photographer J.L.Wood took some splendid photographs of pits and pitmen during the inter-war years. Here, in 1936, the intrepid Wood can be seen ready to be secured to the top of the cage at New Monckton prior to an amazing descent. *J.L.Wood*

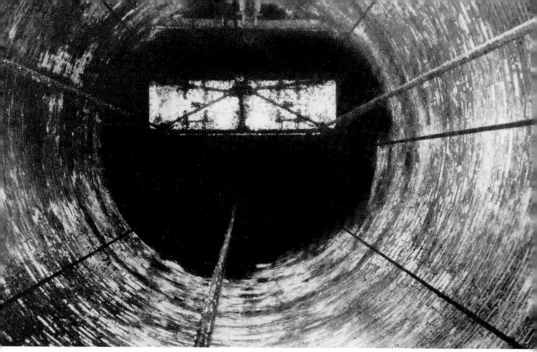

87. The result of Wood's couragous exploit was this exceptional view of the shaft and the ascending cage. *Pit Shaft* succeeded in winning Wood a prestigious photographic award, a proud recognition of his professional skills and ingenuity. *J.L. Wood*

88. Wood also took a series of innovative photographs of Monckton miners, such as this example which gives us a good indication of 1930s working clothes and equipment. *J.L. Wood*

89(a). Two Monckton pit deputies, from the camera of James Wood in 1936. The miner's check belonged to my grandfather, Fred Elliott. *J. L. Wood*

90. One of a fine series of views taken by J. L. Wood showing part of the huge Monckton Colliery complex, in the distance (far left) the pit manager's house. The 'MONCKTON' logo on most of the railway wagons adds interest to the composition. *J. L. Wood*

91. Some children of a miner's family c.1932 when there was widespread poverty in pit communities.

They are four (of nine) children of Fred and Susannah Elliott, nee Firth (my paternal grandparents) who lived at Carlton:

(Left to Right) Audrey (b.1926), Ruby (b.1925), Frank (b.1931) and Joan (b.1928). Fred (1888-1948) was a collier at Monckton.

Daily Herald

No. 6390 · · FRIDAY, AUGUST 7, 1936 ONE PENNY

ALL HOPE FOR 57 PIT VICTIMS ABANDONED

32 BODIES FOUND: GRIM SEARCH GOES ON: ONLY ONE MAN SAVED

AFTER THEIR ORDEAL.—Dr. T. F. Quigley, of Cudworth, and Dr. J. Henderson, of Royston, photographed on their return from the working; and (left) the anxious crowd waiting at the pithead.

ALL hope for the 57 men trapped by the huge explosion in the Lidget seam of Wharncliffe Wood-moor Colliery, Carlton, near Barnsley (South Yorks), has been abandoned. Only one man came out of the pit alive.

Thirty-two bodies have been found and brought to the surface. A grim, silent pilgrimage of death, they were taken through a crowd of a thousand at the pithead to a church schoolroom, where 40 nurses from a ten-miles area are helping the doctors.

And in that crowd were hundreds of

SORROWING CROWD JOINS IN PRAYERS

German
For Spa
Rebe

SECRET CARGO
FRENCH C

From Our Own Co
PARIS, Thursday.

NEWS reached French Ministerial circles tonight that a German steamer is now on its way to Spain with a cargo of 28 bombing planes aboard.

The vessel is the Usaramo, which left Hamburg on July 31. Pilots and mechanics for the planes are on board.

92. Fifty-eight miners lost their lives in the disaster that occurred at Wharncliffe Woodmoor 1, 2 and 3 Colliery, Carlton on 6 August 1936, following an underground explosion (at 3.00 am) in the Lidget workings. This was the dramatic headline of the *Daily Herald* newspaper the following morning. My father (b.1917) worked at this pit at the time of the disaster.

93. The scene at Carlton Board School (later used as a scissors factory and long demolished), Laithes Lane, where the bodies were conveyed (note the ambulance on the right) on that grim summer Thursday in 1936.

94-96. Cover, inside (Order of Service) and back page (list of victims) of the programme of the 'United Memorial Service' held at Barnsley Town Hall a week after the Woodmoor disaster. *NUM*

The Grimethorpe Colliery Band provided the music for the service. Allan Armstrong (b.1925) recently recalled to me how the bellman walked around the village of Grimethorpe 'announcing' the disaster.

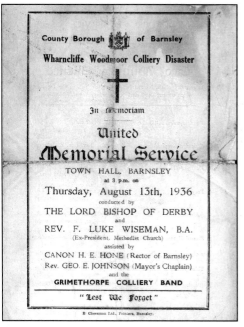

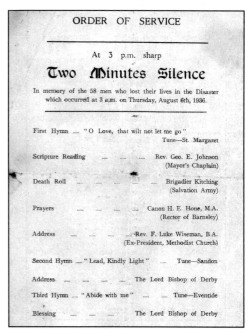

ORDER OF SERVICE

At 3 p.m. sharp

Two Minutes Silence

In memory of the 58 men who lost their lives in the Disaster which occurred at 3 a.m. on Thursday, August 6th, 1936.

First Hymn ..... "O Love, that wilt not let me go" Tune—St. Margaret

Scripture Reading ... ... Rev. Geo. E. Johnson (Mayor's Chaplain)

Death Roll ... ... Brigadier Kitching (Salvation Army)

Prayers .... Canon H. E. Hone, M.A. (Rector of Barnsley)

Address .... Rev. F. Luke Wiseman, B.A. (Ex-President, Methodist Church)

Second Hymn ..... "Lead, Kindly Light" ..... Tune—Sandon

Address .... The Lord Bishop of Derby

Third Hymn ..... "Abide with me" .... Tune—Eventide

Blessing .... The Lord Bishop of Derby

County Borough of Barnsley

Wharncliffe Woodmoor Colliery Disaster

In memoriam

United Memorial Service

TOWN HALL, BARNSLEY

at 3 p.m. on

Thursday, August 13th, 1936

conducted by

THE LORD BISHOP OF DERBY

and

REV. F. LUKE WISEMAN, B.A.

(Ex-President, Methodist Church)

assisted by

CANON H. E. HONE (Rector of Barnsley)

Rev. GEO. E. JOHNSON (Mayor's Chaplain)

and the

GRIMETHORPE COLLIERY BAND

" Lest We Forget "

B. Chessman Ltd., Printers, Barnsley.

Lest We Forget

In Memoriam

In affectionate memory of the following, all of whom lost their lives in the Wharncliffe Woodmoor Colliery Disaster, on Thursday, August 6th, 1936.

John William Harold Abbott	Benjamin Hodgson
Walter Allott	John Edward Hopes
Cleasby Bailey	Enoch Hulson
William Arthur Bateman	Charles Edward Ismay
Arthur Bird	John Jackson
Henry Birkhead	John David Jones
Lewis Boyd	Samuel Kirk
Alfred Brown	Henry Lee
John Brown	James Robert Miller
Samuel Brown	Owen Owens
William Buckley	Hiram Clarence Parkin
John Bullington	James William Poole
Cecil Chapman	William Proctor
Victor Clarkson	John Roscoe
Frederick Cooper	Harold Rowe
Ernest Dalby	Ernest Scargill
John Donelly	William Henry Senior
Walter Duerden	Joseph Thomas Smith
William Alfred Ellis	Walter Smith
George Farmery	Alexander George Henry Thompson
John Fletcher	George Thompson
Irvin Foster	William Alfred Tompkins
James Green	Herbert Travis
Richard Brookes Grimshaw	John Waugh
Frank Hadfield	Archie White
Arthur Molineaux Haigh	William Whiteley
Herbert Hall	George Henry Wilson
Harry Hatfield	Harry Wright
Horace Llewellyn Hepworth	Richard Wright

97. Proudly wearing badges, the Yorkshire Miners' Delegates at the TUC conference in Brighton, September 1933. Herbert Smith (centre with his cap placed under his chair), the most prominent figure.

Left to right, they are: (back row) S. Foster, H. Adwick, T. Briggs, W. Dimelaw and C. Butterwood; (front row) H. Ross, H. Curry, F. Williams, H.(?) Hough, Herbert Smith, J. Jones, A. Smith and J.D. Plant. *NUM*

98. A superb self-portrait by Woolley collier and photographer Irvin Harris (1912-98), c.1937. He would have used a long exposure lit by the light on his helmet. *Harris Collection*

Chapter Three
1941-1960 : Nationalisation and Robens

99. Albert Laister (b.1899), miners' union secretary at Rockingham Main. From one of a series of sketches produced for *Coal Magazine* by H.R.Freeth c.1948. *A.K. Clayton*

100. A VIP visit to Wharncliffe Woodmoor 1, 2 and 3 Colliery, 3 October 1943. General Sir Ralph Eastwood (centre, Commanding Officer, Northern Command) and (Left to Right) Ald. J. Walton, Ald. S. Trueman (Mayor of Barnsley) and Mr J.W. Cook, colliery manager.

101. A group of 'Bevin Boys' photographed in 1943. The scheme, which received a great deal of publicity, involved recruitment of young men of 'call-up' age – by ballot. After training, relatively few reached the coal face but many lads were responsible for valuable work in, for example, underground haulage and pit top work. A number of Bevin Boy songs survive, one of the repeatable ones (sung to the tune of *Paper Doll*) as follows:

> *As I walked down the street the other day,*
> *A damsel turned to me and she did say:*
> *'Why aren't you in kharki or navy blue*
> *And fighting for your country like other boys do?'*
> *I turned to her and and this I did reply.*
> *The answer nearly made the poor girl cry!*
> *'The army I have tried to join.*
> *But Bevin sent me down the mine*
> *And left me with a broken heart.'*

102. On 21 June 1947, Prime Minister Clement Attlee and minister of Power Emannual ('Manny') Shimwell were in Barnsley as speakers and guests of the Yorkshire Miners' Gala. Before the march to Locke Park they were given a civic welcome at the Town Hall by the Mayor, Charles Bentley and Town Clerk, A.E. Gilfillan.

103. As from 1 January 1947, or 'Vesting Day' the new National Coal Board under the chairmanship of Lord Hyndley took control of the country's 1,647 mines, along with a million acres of land, 100,000 dwellings and other facilities formerly in private hands. Coal owners were paid £164.6 million in compensation. *NUM*

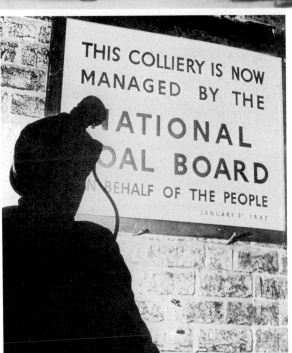

104. Two colliers celebrating 'FIRST NATIONAL COAL' cut on 1 January 1947. The NCB wanted to increase coal production but in the context of reducing the miners' week to five days, improving working conditions and extending fringe benefits. This policy – welcomed by the Union – was reversed by the Conservative Thatcher administration during the 1980s when closing so-called uneconomic pits and making so many mineworkers unemployed. *NUM*

105. A dead miner is carried on a stretcher from Barnsley Main watched by *Barnsley Chronicle* journalist Cyril Kilner. Nine men were killed on Wednesday 7 May 1947, following an explosion in No. 3 District. Joe Hall commented that in his experience of 36 pit disasters there 'has never been less trouble in getting men and getting them away to the first aid stations established at the pit bottom and on the top'; but found 'my old friend' Harry Storey (an experienced rescue team leader) 'knocked out' on the pit bottom, and despite artificial respiration poor Harry was 'dead before we got to the top.'

106. In 1951 (Saturday 25 August) two Swedish women were given permission to visit Dearne Valley Colliery. Here are the party on the pit top before going underground: (Left to Right) Arthur Craven, Bob Craven, Miss Mavis Sharp, Colin Massingham, Britta Gejer (Swedish), Mrs Laura Smith, Ulla Britt Barbara- Awling (Swedish), Ben Nichols and Bill Smith. *Colin Massingham*

107. Two eighteen year old miners – Jonathan Smales and Thomas Cassidy (and their racing whippets 'Oxo', 'Baski' and 'Rosebud') - pause for a national newspaper's photographer, pit in the background, during the so-called Grimethorpe 'stint strike' of 1947.

The dispute began when the colliers' stint in a seam at Grimethorpe was unreasonably increased from 21 feet to 23 feet. *Daily Mirror/Johnny Wood*

108. The former Wharncliffe Woodmoor 4 and 5 miner Roy Mason (centre) on the terrace of the House of Commons in 1953. At the age of 29 he had become Barnsley's youngest-ever Member of Parliament, gaining the support of the Yorkshire Miners' Parliamentary Panel and local Labour Party.

109. A c1960 advertisement for 'Lumax' bulbs by Ceag Ltd of Barnsley, makers of the 'world renown' miner's lamp.

110 & 111. Two fine
photographs by Irvin
Harris showing colliers
cutting coal at the
North Thorncliffe
seam, Woolley c.1948.
Harris Collection

112. Another superb Irvin Harris photograph with lots of atmosphere: shot firing at
Woolley Colliery, c1952. *Harris Collection*

113. Pit pony stalls at Woolley c1950. The pit cat was an essential 'employee' to keep rats and mice at bay. *Harris Collection*

114. 'Charlie' in his well-kept underground stable, Woolley Colliery, 1950s. Ponies were given the considerable protection of the 1911 *Coal Mines Act* and generally speaking horsekeepers took great pride in their ponies, usually the charge of a pony lad – who had to deal with animals of varying temperaments.

As a boy I remember feeding ponies that had been put outside in fields near Carlton (Wharncliffe Woodmoor 1, 2 and 3) pit during the summer holidays *Johnny Wood*

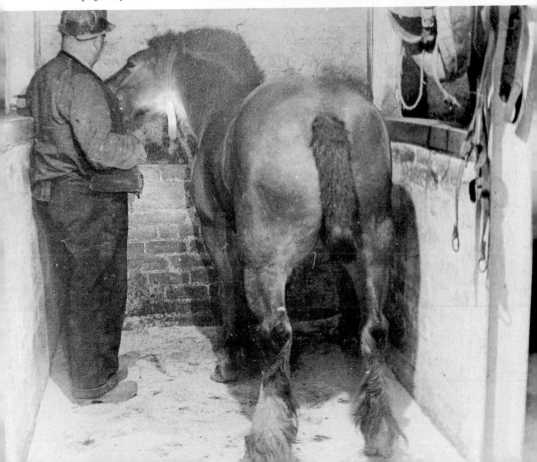

115. The Yorkshire Area NUM Executive Committee photographed by J.R. Roberts of Barnsley in 1958. **Back row** (Left to Right): A. Hepworth (staff), D. Sheldon (Highgate), B. Goddard (Houghton Main), J.D. Gray (Ackton Hall), J. Pashley (Micklefield), W. Moorhouse (Newland) and G. Welch (Elsecar). **Middle row:** T. Ryan (Monk Bretton), R. Smith (Denby Grange), E. Young (Treeton), J. Finnie (Thurcroft), T. Burke (Barnburgh), H. Dixon (Wentworth Silkstone), H. Dore (Bullcroft), H. Miles (Monckton 'A'), H. Lockwood (Grange Moor) and A. Smethurst (East Ardsley).

Front row: F. Machin (author), T.H. Ashman (Financial Secretary), S. Bullough (Vice-President), J.R.A. Machin (President), F. Collindridge (General Secretary), J.T. Collins (Compensation Agent) and E. Wainwright (N.E.C. Member).

The group are assembled at the back of the Miners' Hall. Notice the magnificent stone carvings of heavy industry - representing railways, shipbuilding and coal mining - over the archways.

This photograph may have been commissioned for use in Frank Machin's *The Yorkshire Miners* book. *NUM*

116. Full and empty tubs: underground at Barrow Colliery, January 1951. *Harris Collection.*

117. Front cover of Frank Machin's *The Yorkshire Miners*, published by the Yorkshire Area NUM and printed by Albert Taylor & Sons of Wombwell in 1958.

The book (496pp) covers the period from the SYMA's formation in 1858 to 1881 when it merged with its West Yorkshire neighbour.

Unfortunately, a planned second volume did not appear because of Frank's death; but almost forty years later the Union commissioned Carolyn Baylies to research the post 1881 history resulting in *The History of the Yorkshire Miners 1881-1918* (Routledge,1993).

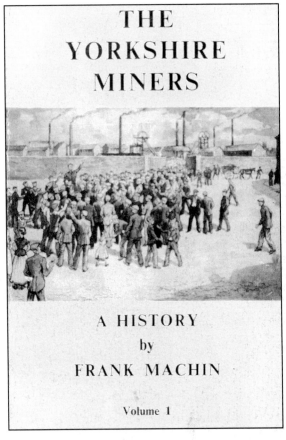

THE
YORKSHIRE
MINERS

A HISTORY
by
FRANK MACHIN

Volume 1

118. Models of a pit tub and miner's electric lamp were presented to Queen Elizabeth II and The Duke of Edinburgh to commemorate their visit to Barnsley on Wednesday 27 October 1954.

119. This junior first-aid team from Grimethorpe Colliery (shown in the background) won the national title in 1960. Seated (Left to Right): Brian Coop (captain), Frederick Waring (instructor) and John Sudworth; standing: Harry Coop (reserve), Geoffrey Ball (reserve), Victor Clarke and Frank Eland. *Ian Walker*

Alfred Robens Plans Personal Probe: Refutes 'Funeral Rites' Rumours

DECENTRALISATION of authority from the centre of command to the point of production was good for everybody concerned, NCB chairman-designate Alfred Robens, MP, said at a Parliamentary Press Gallery lunch. He wished to stop people 'passing the buck.' Those who could not make decisions lower down were the wrong people for the job.

'I am not going to the National Coal Board to direct the funeral rites of this great industry,' Mr. Robens told the corps of Parliamentary newspapermen. 'It is Britain's basic industry. Britain's wealth is based on it, and it is going to be the key industry for this country, so far as it lies within my power.'

Maintaining he was not afraid of change, Mr. Robens said, 'I am sorry that leaders of the miners' union have made up their minds about things so quickly, so much in advance, from information which they may think is perfectly good, but which I can tell them is perfectly bad.

'I realise the job that has to be done in the Coal Board. It is a non-political, business-like job. Therefore, when people talk glibly about decentralisation I sometimes wonder whether they know what they are talking about.

'I have always been a great believer in decentralisation of authority from the centre of command to the point of production. It is good for everybody concerned. There are some vistas of this vast industry where you need to have some decentralised control. It is all a matter of degree.'

To those who would try to alarm workers in the industry by saying there was to be a return to what happened in pre-war years, Mr. Robens replied: 'Surely no one would believe I would take the chairmanship of the National Coal Board and return the coal industry to pre-war days. It is too fantastic to believe that—unless I have been bought for £10,000 a year.

'But my price is very much higher

NCB chairman-designate Alfred Robens. *COAL photo*

than that. I don't know how high it is, but I haven't been offered any more than that.'

Mr. Robens spoke of his wish to stop people 'passing the buck'. 'I don't intend to have my desk littered with papers for my decision. If people cannot themselves make decisions lower down then they are the wrong people. We must get people in who can. They are entitled to make two wrong decisions, but not three.' He was prepared to take the risk of having decisions lower down.

The NCB was such a vast organisation that the chairman did not even know what was going on. 'I want people to make the decisions who do know what is going on.

'I don't know what form of decentralisation is required,' Mr. Robens continued, 'I won't know until I go on the pay-roll, which is not until October 1. From October 1 until February 1, when I take over from Jim Bowman, I don't propose to do any work for my salary.'

120. 'I'm not going to the National Coal Board to direct the funeral rites of this great industry': Alfred Robens, NCB Chairman-Designate, 1960.
He proceeded to close more than 400 pits. *Coal*

Chapter Four
1961-1980 : Pit Closures and Landmark Strikes

121. A group of Barnsley Main deputies waiting to go down the pit for the afternoon shift c.1961.

They are, back row (Left to right):

Jack Drury, Walt Haigh, Bill Price, Frank Mitchell; middle row: Jim Farnsworth, Horace Austin, Eddie Hunter, Sam Brown; front row: Jim Smith and Albert Sykes. *Ken Hindley.*

122. Three miners at Wharncliffe Woodmoor 1, 2 and 3 Colliery c.1962: (Left to Right) Keith Jones, Fred Elliott and Brian Summerfield. The pit was one of the many 'Robens closures' of the mid-1960s, my father (Fred) 'transferring' to a pit-top job at Grimethorpe power station, after more than 40 years working underground.

123. Dodworth (Redbrook Section) brass band rehearse for a pit-bottom carol service in December 1961. Leader Stanley O'Conner is just in view on the left of the photograph. A tradition of underground carol services at Redbrook pit bottom began in the late 1940s. *George Rawson*

124. Grimethorpe miners admire a fine array of first aid trophies placed on display at the pit, 28 May 1961. The First Aid station can be seen in the background. The notice suggests that a new 'Ladies Section' was anticipated. Note the 'snap tin' carried by one of the onlookers. *NCB/Ian Walker*

125. Grimethorpe St John's Ambulance team consisting of: (Left to Right) Albert Yoxall, Fred Waring, Terry Haynes, Eddie Hyde, Ian Walker and Joe Round, are seen here as winners of the huge 'Michael Hedges' trophy which took place in Skegness, 1965. *Ian Walker*

THE 1965 MINERS' GALA IN BARNSLEY

Programme of the Day

10.30 a.m.   **PROCESSION**
through the Town.

11.30 a.m.   **SPEECHES**
in Locke Park.

1.00 p.m.   **CONCERT by the West Riding County Fire Service
Silver Band, Pipes and Corps of Drums**
at the Band Platform and also at :

1.45 p.m.   **MARCHING DISPLAY and "Beat the Retreat"**

2.00 p.m.   **FANCY DRESS SHOW**
at the Band Platform.

3.00 p.m.   **FASHION PARADE**
at Speakers' Platform.

3.00 p.m.   **MASSED BANDS CONCERT**
at the Band Platform.

4.00 p.m.   **COAL QUEEN CONTEST**
at Speakers' Platform.

●

N.C.B. AND S.M.R.E. EXHIBITIONS

ALL DAY :—
The N.C.B. has kindly built in the Park a realistic Coal Face showing the most
modern techniques and with emphasis on Safety. This installation could have
been powered and could operate but, in the interests of public safety, will not be
operated. The Safety in Mines Research Establishment will collaborate with
their own Exhibition.

●

SPECIAL ATTRACTIONS

The Tower in Locke Park will be open to the Public
Children's Roundabout   Children's Playground
Punch and Judy Shows at regular intervals
Balloon Race—Proceeds to Local Charities

FULL MEALS, SNACKS AND LICENSED BAR

Page 14

Programme of Speeches

(Commencing at 11.30 a.m. approximately)

**THE WORSHIPFUL
THE MAYOR OF BARNSLEY**
(Alderman A. Butler, J.P.)
will extend a Civic Welcome to the Assembly

●

CHAIRMAN :
Mr. S. BULLOUGH

SPEAKERS :
Mr. GEORGE BROWN, M.P.
(First Secretary of State)

LORD COLLISON
(Chairman of the Trades Union Congress)

VOTE OF THANKS :
Mr. S. Schofield
Mr. J. Harper, M.P.

●

The Chairman will formally move the Resolution

Page 12

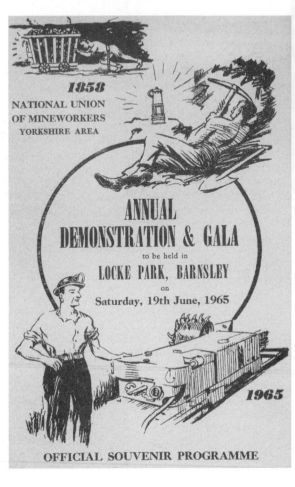

1858

NATIONAL UNION
OF MINEWORKERS
YORKSHIRE AREA

ANNUAL
DEMONSTRATION & GALA
to be held in
LOCKE PARK, BARNSLEY
on
Saturday, 19th June, 1965

1965

OFFICIAL SOUVENIR PROGRAMME

126. Programme cover of the 1965 Yorkshire Miners' Gala, held in Lock Park, Barnsley.

The long procession - which included no less than 46 brass bands headed by a Pipes and Corps of Drums band - started from the Miners' Hall, Victoria Road and simultaneously from Keir Street and Churchfields.
Ron Palmer

127-128. Programme of Events and Programme of Speeches. *Ron Palmer*

129. The Dodworth (Church Lane) branch and Dodworth Miners' Welfare Prize band proudly march along Peel Street in 1965. The marshalls were J. Woffenden and B. Richardson. Mr Ron Palmer (centre, right of St John's Ambulance man) is one of the leaders. 'Unity is Strength' proclaims the old Church Lane banner. Note the size of the crowd lining the street – galas were very popular occasions. *Ron Palmer*

130. Flanked by police officers and a young autograph hunter in pursuit, George Brown MP strides through Locke Park on the way to the Speakers' Platform.

131. Yorkshire Miners' Summer School at Bingley in 1966 when Professor Douglas Jay (seated, arms folded, near centre) was the main speaker. *Ron Palmer*

132. The big push up Blenheim Road towards Park Road, at the 1969 Yorkshire Miners' Gala, when Minister of Fuel & Power, Roy Mason and Lawrence Daly, NUM Secretary were the principal speakers. The banners in the foreground are for the Kellingley and Acton Hall areas. *Roy Portman*

133. 'One World. One Class. One Aim. Socialism in our Time': miners making their way home at the end of the 1969 Yorkshire Miners' Gala. The other banners in view are for Walton and Fryston. *Roy Portman*

Miners in three coalfields may join 70,000 strikers

The Yorkshire coalfield strike, which began yesterday with more than 70,000 miners staying away from work, now seems likely to spread to other areas.

In Scotland, a sympathy strike appeared last night to be imminent; in Wales, where lodges have already suggested strike action, a conference representing 42,000 miners is to meet at Porthcawl today to discuss a claim for shorter hours for surface workers; and in Derbyshire, Mr. Herbert Parkin, secretary of the Derbyshire N.U.M., said yesterday that unrest among his 17,000 members had reached explosive level.

PICKET MEETING

Miners from Yorkshire are to picket the meeting of Derbyshire Miners' Council today. The Derbyshire men decided a week ago that if the issue of working hours for surface men was not settled, industrial action should be considered today.

The Scottish position was outlined yesterday after a meeting in Edinburgh of the Scottish area of the NUM. Mr. Michael McGahey, president of the Scottish NUM, said that pithead meetings were being called to test the feeling of the men, and the decision would be taken by a special delegate conference.

"I think it is inevitable that there will be a strike," he said, "unless the Coal Board is prepared to accede to the union's demands." Many of the men in Scotland were in a militant mood, he added, and he would not be surprised if action was taken at individual pits before the delegate conference was held.

The industry in Scotland now employs 30,500 members at 34 pits.

The Yorkshire miners, whose unofficial strike on its first day closed all but two of the coalfield's 75 pits, will fight to the finish, said their leader, Mr. Sam Bullough, at Barnsley last night. Mr. Bullough, Yorkshire area president of the National Union of Mineworkers, said: "The men are very angry, and I can see no break in the strike."

The strike in Yorkshire is in support of the NUM demands for a working week of 40 hours, including meal breaks, for all surface men. The Coal Board has offered 40 hours excluding meal breaks. Only at Parkhill Colliery, Wakefield, where the union branch decided on Sunday night not to strike, and at Water Haigh Colliery, near Leeds, was there partial working yesterday.

News that the dayshift was working at Parkhill quickly attracted pickets from other collieries. The afternoon shift, said one Parkhill miner, "turned round and went home like lambs when they met the pickets."

SOME BITTER

Some Parkhill men were bitter about the presence of the pickets. Their colliery has mining problems, and they fear that a strike there would only hasten any Coal Board decision to close it. But Councillor W. O'Brien, secretary of the North Yorkshire Panel of the NUM, told the Parkhill miners: "We have lived so long as mice that the Coal Board will still close pits, strike or not." Parkhill, if it continued working, would be "the first colliery to be attacked by the Coal Board because it is weak and the Coal Board will know it."

The Yorkshire Area Council of the NUM has written to its national executive committee, giving the reasons for the strike but not asking for it to be made official. Until it is made official there will be no strike pay for the Yorkshire miners.

Mr. Jack Leigh, the vice-president, said that the men would not go back to work "until they get something tangible." Everybody in the coalfield knew that coal was fighting for its existence, but the Yorkshire miners had reached the end of the road.

Yorkshire miners who visited the headquarters of the Nottinghamshire Miners' Council at Berry Hill, Mansfield, were given a hearing by the Notts executive but told that Nottinghamshire would proceed through constitutional channels.

One of the visitors, commenting on the meeting, said afterwards that the Yorkshire miners would decide whether or not to organise picketing at Nottinghamshire pits.

134. The growing concern over pay, working hours and conditions; and of course an increasing number of pit closures, led to the kind of unofficial strike action reported in this extract from the *Guardian* newspaper of 14 October 1969. *NUM*

135. In 1969 Woolley Colliery celebrated its centenary, marked by this souvenir NCB booklet.

In the same year the pit produced a million tons of coal for the first time, doubling 'shift worked' productivity since nationalization - with 500 fewer men employed.

The pit manager was George Duncan and the NUM officials included Alvin Philips, Elijah Benn, Arthur Scargill and Godfrey Sunderland.

In later years, as with many other Barnsley pits, a massive amount of investment was made, including building the huge washery complex, an unmistakable landmark when seen from the M1 motorway, but Woolley closed in 1987.

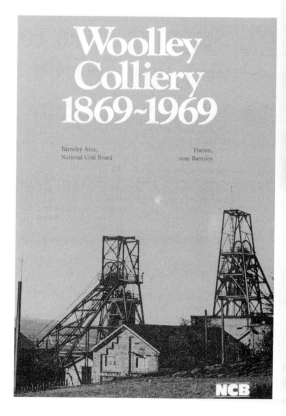

Woolley Colliery 1869~1969

Barnsley Area, National Coal Board

Darton, near Barnsley

NCB

136. Travelling on the pit paddy at Woolley c.1969.

137-138. The NCB offices at Grimethorpe, pit and power station in the background;and the Grimethorpe & Ferrymoor Miners' Welfare & Institute, both photographs dating from 1969. *Angela Elliott*

139-41. Tickets for three Sixties NCB social events.
(1) Dance at the Civic Hall, Barnsley;
(2) Dance at Arcadian Hall, Barnsley; and
(3)Beat Ball at Cudworth. *Terry Bowman*

NATIONAL COAL BOARD—No. 4 (Carlton) Area
Area Headquarters Staff

ANNUAL DANCE

Civic Hall, Barnsley

FRIDAY, 29th NOVEMBER, 1963
from 8 p.m. to 1 a.m.

GEOFF HAIGH ORCHESTRA

Licensed Bar   Dress Optional

6/-   ADMISSION BY TICKET ONLY

NATIONAL COAL BOARD
No. 4 (Carlton) Area

AREA HEADQUARTERS

ANNUAL SPRING DANCE

in the ARCADIAN HALL, BARNSLEY

FRIDAY, 1st MAY, 1964
from 8 p.m. to 1 a.m.

LICENSED BAR   DRESS OPTIONAL
LATE TRANSPORT

THE JOHNNY JOHNSTON QUINTET
"UNIT 4" RHYTHM GROUP

6/-   Admission by Ticket Only

NATIONAL COAL BOARD
No. 4 AREA STAFF

BEAT BALL

at

CUDWORTH VILLAGE CLUB
on
14th. February 1964
DANCING   8 to 12

ADMISSION   5/-

142. Children playing by the backs of typical miners' terrace (Lanky Row, Hawshaw Lane) at Hoyland Common, shortly before demolition in July 1967. *A.K.Clayton*

143. A good view of the main buildings at Elsecar Main in 1969. Sunk in c1908, winding coal c.1910, the pit closed and the buildings demolished in 1985. A competition was held for the prize winner 'to blow up' the big chimney. *A.K.Clayton*

144. Once such a common sight: a load of coal covering part of the causeway and street, after delivery to a property in Beaumont Street, Hoyland Common, August 1971.
A.K.Clayton

145. Another rare sight: one of the last cast iron ranges, from a property in Kay Street Hoyland Common, 1973.

146. Lord Robens on an official visit to the Grimethorpe Ambulance Station, probably as part of the pit village gala day, 3 July 1971.

The group consists of (Left to Right): Frank Ramsden (pit manager), Harry Nettleton (Councillor), Lord Alfred Robens (Chairman of NCB), George Dean, Eric Brown, Michael Eaton (NCB Area Director) and Norman Stacey (Councillor). *Ian Walker/NCB*

147-148. Cheers! Christening the new canteen at Redbrook pit, 1970.

With the canteen manageress on the exterior photograph are (Left to Right): Don Jagger (NUM Sec) and Ron Palmer (NUM Treasurer). *NCB/Ron Palmer*

"KEEP COOL" APPEALS TO PICKETS

Strike battlefield violence grows

by Frazer Wright, Industrial Correspondent. Morning Telegraph

AS VIOLENCE gripped miners' picket lines yesterday, there were growing fears among their leaders that troops might be called in to maintain coal supplies, and officially to break the pickets' stranglehold on power stations and fuel depots.

Yesterday's picket battlefields were the two South Yorkshire pits of Kilnhurst and Cadeby, and again, a Gas Board coke depot in Birmingham, where today's confrontation between police, lorry drivers and pickets is being forecast as the main "showdown" of the strike so far.

In South Yorkshire, colliery officials were again the targets for the pickets. There were arrests at both pits. A car was overturned, five others had tyres deflated and valves cut, a pit manager was threatened by a picket in his own office, colliery windows were smashed, and a pit undermanager was "man-handled" by pickets.

Birmingham police has been put on an emergency two-shift system, involving four hours extra duty for hundreds of men, in case of further trouble at the West Midlands Gas Board depot at Saltley which holds the last big coke stocks in the Midlands.

Nearly 500 Yorkshire and Derbyshire pickets took part in the Birmingham picket yesterday. There were allegations last night from one of their leaders, Mr. Arthur Scargill, that police had used excessive brutality to keep the depot open.

SHOWDOWN

"I am black and blue, like most of the other Barnsley pickets. We have been kicked to death by policemen standing four or five deep," he claimed.

Three hundred police tried to hold back pickets as lorries from all parts of Britain queued at the gates. The first clashes came when two lorries broke through the picket lines. A young policeman was punched in the stomach and taken to hospital. Twenty pickets were arrested.

Mr. Scargill said: "We are expecting Tuesday to be the showdown. We have called for picket reinforcements from Scotland and Yorkshire. We are determined to shut this blacklegging depot."

Transport workers have joined the picket lines and, he added, two local factories had walked out on strike to join the lines.

There was now a very real fear that troops would be called in to help the police. "We heard the police themselves asking for this help on their inter com systems," said Mr. Scargill.

Barnsley MP Mr. Roy Mason, a former Minister of Power, called for the closing of the depot to all but essential traffic—"or clashes with the police will be inevitable."

He hoped the pickets would act responsibly—an appeal echoed by Rother Valley MP Mr. Peter Hardy who said: "We are in a situation where violence is bubbling near the surface." He urged pickets: "Keep your cool!"

Mr. Leslie Huckfield, MP for Nuneaton, is to ask the Home Secretary today to investigate police behaviour in the clashes.

At Barnsley, Yorkshire NUM secretary Mr. Sidney Schofield said: "We are making preparations for a long and bitter battle if that is necessary."

Delegates to the Yorkshire area NUM council urged their national executive to ban all safety work, and to press colliery officials to do the same.

149. The report, taken from the (Sheffield) *Morning Telegraph* concerns the February 1972 miners' strike, Frazer Wright making reference to the 'picket battlefields' at the Gas Board coke depot, Saltley which held 'the last big stocks in the Midlands'.

150. Mass, strategic but responsible pickets, as can be seen in the photograph, resulted in support from workers in Birmingham and the police closing the works. The Government set up the Wilberforce Inquiry into miners' wages, eventually resulting in a significant pay settlement. 'Saltley Gate' was a landmark victory for the miners' union. *NUM*

151. The saddest moment of the 1972 strike was the death of Hatfield Main picket Fred Matthews and his funeral at Hatfield, attended by an estimated 10,000 crowd of Yorkshire miners and miners' families as well as representatives from other coalfield areas. Fred was crushed to death by a lorry outside Keadby Power Station. *Ron Palmer/NUM*

Coal strike:
Yorkshire's Yes beats national poll

by Glen Allan and Robin Morgan. Yorkshire Post

AT LEAST three out of every four miners who voted in last week's pithead ballot are believed to have supported strike action.

The total poll is put at 75 per cent of the National Union of Mineworkers' 250,000 members.

In Yorkshire the vote is said to show more than 80 per cent in favour of strike action.

Another estimate put the vote in Yorkshire as high as 90 per cent overall with many pits reporting almost unanimous votes in favour of a strike.

Branch officials at pits throughout the coalfield were forecasting majorities from between 98 and 80 per cent.

Nottinghamshire is reported to have returned a substantial strike vote for the first time in its history. It is regarded as one of the most moderate of the NUM areas.

There must be 55 per cent in favour of strike action before the NUM executive can halt the pits.

The result will be announced officially by Mr. Joe Gormley, NUM president, this morning.

The count was completed at the Electoral Reform Society's Southwark, London, headquarters last night.

Maj. Frank Britton, the society's controller of ballot services, will hand his written report to the NUM at the union's headquarters in London's Euston Road in time for an announcement at 10 a.m.

Referring to his "deadline" for receipt of ballot papers Maj. Britton said he now believed all voting papers that were expected had arrived safely.

The 27-man executive of the NUM meets tomorrow to consider future action in the light of the ballot result. It is expected to decide on a strike date, but much may depend on the Heath-TUC talks.

If the last ditch efforts fail the strike is almost certain to start next weekend.

But there are bound to be objections from the moderates on the NUM executive both on the timing of the strike and on the form which it would take.

Mr. Gormley said yesterday that any decision to call a strike would be "sooner rather than later." He was fed up with "abortive talks."

Then he added: "But if we are in the middle of negotiations or there is hope of things being settled . . . nobody is going to start shouting the odds to start a strike at that time."

Mr. Gormley said it was essential for the miners to be awarded the "right wage" this year. Members were convinced that if they were not given it "they are not going to get it any other year."

Mr. Gormley hit out at the idea of setting up of a new review board to examine the miners' pay claim.

"Are they going to convince the miners that the board will deal with their arguments any differently than the Pay Board dealt with the arguments?" he said.

"This is asking us to look stupid in the minds of our own members."

Asked if he saw any solution through the relativities procedure, he replied: "I am ruling out nothing. I want honestly to find a solution to the problem, but it must be a solution to the problem that can be honourably accepted by the membership of the NUM and be honourably accepted by the Government if they want honourably to accept it.

"I don't give a damn whether they call it within Phase Three, within Phase 23 or within the relativity agreement."

152-153. A report of 4 February 1974 concerning the NUM pithead ballot indicating a very convincing 'Yes' vote in favour of strike action at a time when pay 'phases' and 'relativities' continued to be insisted on by the Heath Government; and a group of Redbrook miners 'VOTE YES'.

154. Arthur Scargill, Mick McGahey and Eric Clark leaving a negotiating meeting with the NCB in 1974.

155-156. Peaceful pickets outside Rockingham Main Colliery, 28 February and on a cold 1 March 1974. *A.K.Clayton*

Houghton Main Colliery
District Plan Showing Incident Detail

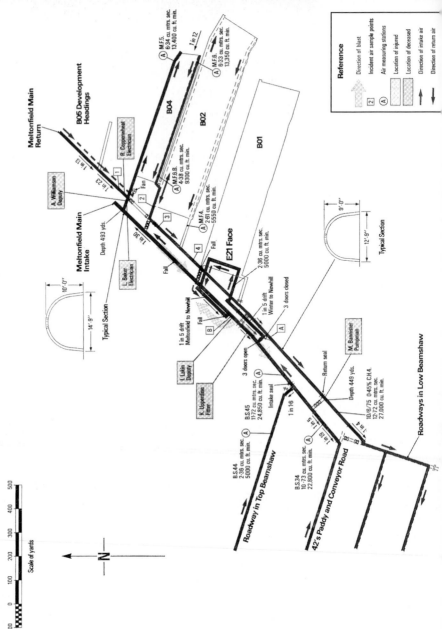

157. Five men (Richard Bannister, Irvin Lakin, Arnold Williamson, Raymond Copperwheat and Leonard Baker) were killed in a violent explosion in the Newhill seam at Houghton Main Colliery, Little Houghton on Thursday 12 June 1975. Another man (Ken Upperdine) received serious burns and five others suffered shock and minor injuries. Yorkshire Miners' President Arthur Scargill, Secretary Owen Briscoe and other NUM officials demanded a public inquiry into the disaster when Energy Secretary Tony Benn and NCB Chairman Sir Derek Ezra visited the pit on the Friday. The Health and Safety Executive's official report (1976) concluded that the explosion 'resulted from the ignition of an accumulation of firedamp in B 05's return development heading which had been unventilated for a period of nine days prior to the explosion.' The 'likely source' being a frictional spark from the impeller and casing of the Carter Howden auxiliary fan. The 'District Plan' was published to show the 'Incident Detail'.
HMSO/Johnny Wood

158. Miners coming off shift at Houghton Main in 1979.

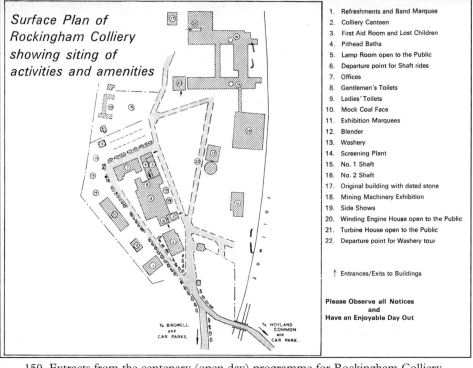

Surface Plan of
Rockingham Colliery
showing siting of
activities and amenities

1. Refreshments and Band Marquee
2. Colliery Canteen
3. First Aid Room and Lost Children
4. Pithead Baths
5. Lamp Room open to the Public
6. Departure point for Shaft rides
7. Offices
8. Gentlemen's Toilets
9. Ladies' Toilets
10. Mock Coal Face
11. Exhibition Marquees
12. Blender
13. Washery
14. Screening Plant
15. No. 1 Shaft
16. No. 2 Shaft
17. Original building with dated stone
18. Mining Machinery Exhibition
19. Side Shows
20. Winding Engine House open to the Public
21. Turbine House open to the Public
22. Departure point for Washery tour

↑ Entrances/Exits to Buildings

Please Observe all Notices
and
Have an Enjoyable Day Out

To BIRDWELL
and
CAR PARKS.

To HOYLAND
COMMON
and
CAR PARK.

159. Extracts from the centenary (open day) programme for Rockingham Colliery, 31 March (Easter Monday) 1975. It was in December 1872 that Earl Fitzwilliam leased 800 acres of coal to Thorncliffe partners, Newton and Chambers, giving them six months 'to prove the coal'. Sinking began in the summer of 1873, the principal seams (Silkstone & Parkgate) reached in the Spring and Autumn of 1875, and the new colliery named 'Rockingham' in honour of the Marquis of Rockingham and the Fitzwilliam family. In his programme notes Colliery General Manager Stanley Collinson refers to the 'ups and downs' of the colliery's fortunes, mainly because of geological problems, but anticipated a high level of production in its centenary year. The pit survived for a further four years.

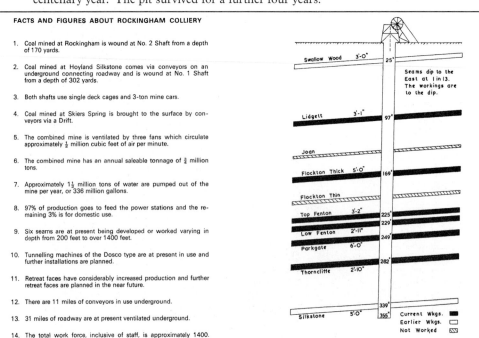

FACTS AND FIGURES ABOUT ROCKINGHAM COLLIERY

1. Coal mined at Rockingham is wound at No. 2 Shaft from a depth of 170 yards.

2. Coal mined at Hoyland Silkstone comes via conveyors on an underground connecting roadway and is wound at No. 1 Shaft from a depth of 302 yards.

3. Both shafts use single deck cages and 3-ton mine cars.

4. Coal mined at Skiers Spring is brought to the surface by conveyors via a Drift.

5. The combined mine is ventilated by three fans which circulate approximately ½ million cubic feet of air per minute.

6. The combined mine has an annual saleable tonnage of ¾ million tons.

7. Approximately 1½ million tons of water are pumped out of the mine per year, or 336 million gallons.

8. 97% of production goes to feed the power stations and the remaining 3% is for domestic use.

9. Six seams are at present being developed or worked varying in depth from 200 feet to over 1400 feet.

10. Tunnelling machines of the Dosco type are at present in use and further installations are planned.

11. Retreat faces have considerably increased production and further retreat faces are planned in the near future.

12. There are 11 miles of conveyors in use underground.

13. 31 miles of roadway are at present ventilated underground.

14. The total work force, inclusive of staff, is approximately 1400.

15. In the early days the work force consisted of mainly local people, but now some men travel from a radius of up to 10 miles.

Swallow Wood 3'-0" 25'

Seams dip to the East at 1 in 13. The workings are to the dip.

Lidgett 3'-1" 97'

Joan

Flockton Thick 5'-0" 169'

Flockton Thin

Top Fenton 3'-2" 225'
229'

Low Fenton 2'-11" 249'

Parkgate 6'-0"
282'

Thorncliffe 2'-10"

339'
Silkstone 5'-0" 355'

Current Wkgs. ■
Earlier Wkgs. □
Not Worked ▨

Shaft Section showing Coal Seams.

160. 'THE LAST TON OF COAL' is inscribed in chalk on the side of a wagon on the last day of production at Rockingham Colliery in November 1979. Among those in the photograph are Dennis Smith, Bill Kelk, David Grafton and Bill Hawksworth. *A.K.Clayton*

161. Rockingham Colliery: probably No.1 pit headgear, September 1973. *A.K. Clayton*

Headgear pulleys in Halves up to 20 feet diameter,
to latest N.C.B. specifications

For new installations, and reconstruction of existing
installations when shafts are due for replacement

NEEDHAM BROTHERS & BROWN LTD

Have specialised in the manufacture of headgear pulleys since 1890

162. The c1960s catalogue cover for Needham Brothers & Brown Ltd, 'manufacturers of headgear pulleys since 1890'. After 118 years, Needhams' assets went under the auctioneer's hammer in October 1994, an obvious casualty of British Coal's pit closure programmes of the 1980s and early 1990s. *Roy Portman*

163. Casting a pulley, using ladles - always a spectacular event at the Needham Bros Foundry, 1977. *Roy Portman*

164. Workers at Needhams marking out the bore on a headgear pulley, mid-1970s. *Roy Portman*

165. A finished twenty-foot pulley wheel leaving the Needham Bros engineering works, Pontefract Road, Barnsley, bound for a NCB colliery. *Roy Portman*

166. Headgear and surface buildings at Skiers Spring Colliery, March 1976. It was Sunk in 1916, but about five years later linked underground to Rockingham, thereafter functioning as a man-riding pit. *A.K.Clayton*

167. A drift mine was opened at Skiers Spring in about 1952. Here, Robert Oxspring (L) and Ron Morris are seen leaving the drift on 1 July 1976. *A.K. Clayton*

168. A cheerful group of Dodworth miners about to get in the cage and descend the shaft in 1978. The 'regulation' clothes provided by the NCB contrast to those worn by earlier generations of pitmen. *Ron Palmer*

169. An old style and modern miner compare clothes and equipment by the side of a kibble at Barnsley Main c.1980 *W. Hollins*

170. Barrow Colliery at Worsbrough Bridge was able to celebrate a century of coal production in 1977 with an open day. Three shafts had been sunk in 1875. In the late Seventies the pit employed 1,536 men, producing 272,000 tonnes pa from mechanized workings in the Swallow Wood and Silkstone seams. Barrow closed a few months after the end of the 1984/85 strike. *A.K. Clayton*

171. The St John's Ambulance Brigade (representing Grimethorpe Colliery) were so successful at a 1978 first-aid competition held in London that they won every trophy. They are (Left to Right): Ian Walker, Mick Green, Trevor Knight, Jimmy Whitehead, Joe Round, Mick Hayes (manager), Terry Haynes and Eddie Hyde (team captain). *NCB/Ian Walker*

172. Miners from Hatfield Main parade their 'Keir Hardie' banner in Barnsley at the 1979 Yorkshire miners' gala. *Dave Douglass*

173. Shorter Day... Better Conditions... Longer Life... . A happy group of miners – and MP Allen McKay (centre) – celebrate the new banner of the Church Lane (Dodworth) Branch in 1980. This photograph was taken at Churchfields, Barnsley, the traditional meeting place where Sections assembled before marching through the town and on to Locke Park during Galas. NUM Union official Mr J. Woffenden is pictured on the banner (see below). *Ron Palmer*

174. Presentation of an Ashley Jackson watercolour painting to retiring and much respected Dodworth official Jack Woffenden, c.1976: (Left to Right) Councillor J. Herrin, Ron Palmer (NUM), Gary Woffenden (NUM), Jack Woffenden (NUM) and Jack Leigh (NUM). *Ron Palmer*

Chapter Five
1981-2000 : FIGHTING FOR JOBS AND COMMUNITIES

175. Grimethorpe miners celebrate a million tonnes of coal production in 1980. The photograph includes Nigel Clark, Mick Brown, Alan Whitely, Steven Logan, Russell Mason and Terry Haynes. The NCB gave a key ring and Parker pen to all men employed at the colliery. *NCB/Johnny Wood*

176. A group of four Cubans pause for an official photograph alongside NUM officials following an underground visit to Woolley Colliery c.1980: Back row (Left to Right): Ralph Summerfield, Cuban woman, Cuban man, Cuban woman, Bruce Hirst and (? production manager); front row: Cuban, Arthur Scargill, Ray Horbury and Ian Barr (pit manager). *NCB/Ralph Summerfield.*

177. The Woolley Branch NUM and Yorkshire Miners' President Arthur Scargill demonstrating in support of nurses, outside Barnsley & District General Hospital, 22 September 1982. Ralph Summerfield is on the right of the photograph and Gary Miller in the centre. *Martin Jenkinson, photographer.*

178. The Yorkshire miners' convalescent home at Scalby, near Scarborough, formerly owned by the Quaker Rowntree family of York. This assembly of union officials were in attendance to celebrate its refurbishment in the early 1980s.

The front row (Left to Right) includes John Walsh (3rd), Sammy Thompson (5), Owen Briscoe (7) Ken Homer (9). Various other officials in view include Frank Cave, Kevin Barron, Ralph Summerfield, Derek Patchet, Derek Reeves, Dave Douglass... *Ralph Summerfield*

179. The distinctive banner of the Hatfield Main NUM branch assemble at the start of the 'Peoples March for Jobs' in 1983. The number of miners employed in the Barnsley area had declined to less than 15,000 and, in March, UK unemployment stood at a record 3.2 million. *Dave Douglass/Martin Jenkinson*

180. The Executive Committee of the Yorkshire NUM in the new meeting room at the Miners' offices, Barnsley c.1981. Representatives from Barnsley, South Yorkshire, North Yorkshire and Doncaster Areas in attendance.

At the head of the table, at the centre, sits President Arthur Scargill; to his left Jack Taylor and Doug Fellowes (staff), and to his right Ken Homer. On the far, long side of the table (Left to Right) sits A. Young, Ralph Summerfield, Derick Reeves, Terry Patchett, Gordon Dixon, Brian Conley, Inkie Thomson, Wilf. Garside and Frank Cave; and on the near side, John Walsh, Derek France, Alan Gosling, Kevin Barron Geoff Turp, (?), Steve Withrington. End of table: Ron Booker, Arthur Gill. *Dave Douglass/NUM*

NOTTS APPEAL

Nottinghamshire miners' leaders Ray Chadburn and Henry Richardson have made a special appeal to their members:

'The strike over pit closures is not just a fight on behalf of Scotland, Yorkshire, the North East, South Wales, Kent or any other areas. It is our fight too.

'For as sure as night follows day, once the Coal Board have wrecked those areas they will start the wholesale butchery of our own coalfield. And when that day dawns who will be around to fight for us?

'Already 2,900 jobs are being cut in South Notts this year alone; and a further reduction of ½m tonnes of capacity is planned. The knock-on effect in the workshops, administration, garages, etc. will be devastating.

'We appeal to our members to get off their knees and fight before it's too late. Not just for today's jobs, but for our future generations.

'We are all miners and we are in the same battle. Stand erect and don't cross picket lines and we shall win the human right to a decent and secure future.'

WANTED: A LIVING

BY NUM PRESIDENT ARTHUR SCARGILL

NUM solidarity is growing rapidly both within the union and among the wider labour and trade union movement.

Massive support is being given by the transport unions, including rail and road, to halt the movement of coal.

The National Union of Seamen have stopped coal imports and all transport unions are now responding to our call to block the movement of fuel oil.

Whole communities — employed and unemployed — miners' wives, the young and old, all are mobilising in an unprecedented display of support.

The Labour Party has publicly declared its backing for the NUM, and the TUC has indicated its willingness to give support when the union requests it.

It has now become clear that MacGregor is acting as the agent of the Tory Government as they push ahead with a bid to close pits and destroy jobs.

His statement on ITV that he wouldn't be against using troops to beat the miners' strike is the clearest indication yet that the fight is not just against the NCB puppets, but the government string-pullers, too.

MacGregor's enthusiasm for the use of troops smacks of what happened in the United States where arms were used against American miners on strike. Obviously, as former head of the US mining company Amax, he believes that such bully tactics can intimidate British miners.

But I am convinced that his attitude will harden the resolve of our membership.

SCARE TACTICS

His latest scare tactic is to say that the strike will make pits unworkable. He knows that the NUM has no objection to senior management doing essential maintenance and to claim otherwise is both silly and an indication of how far the Board will go in its propaganda war.

It should never be forgotten that it was the Coal Board which broke off communications with the union and have refused to hold talks ever since. MacGregor will not debate the issues publicly, refusing to appear on live TV with me. The explanation is simple — it would give the British people an opportunity to see that the Coal Board haven't a case.

MacGregor's record speaks for itself. At British Steel in just three years he cut jobs from 166,400 to 81,000, while the loss per worker actually rose from £3,293 to £4,759.

But all this means nothing unless we understand one essential fact. The ultimate aim, as Industry Secretary Norman Tebbit admitted last week, is to sell off our biggest money makers. Tebbit said:

"I wonder whether we would have a coal mining dispute if we had denationalised the coal industry 10 or 20 years ago. It is a thought for the future."

Meanwhile, the dispute so far has cost the British tax payer a heavy price. Over £850m has been eaten up in 18 million tonnes of lost production.

INVINCIBLE

The para-military police operation in Nottinghamshire and the Midlands is estimated at £2 million per day — clocking up £75 million so far. It has cost the CEGB a further £75m in just five weeks to burn oil instead of coal.

Thus the total cost of our action is £1000m, or six times the cash subsidies needed to keep open the pits immediately threatened.

I emphasise that the miners of our country are fighting for the very survival of coal and, indeed, for the industrial base of Britain.

With unity, determination and commitment, our union is invincible.

I call on every member to do everything in his power to defend pits and jobs.

Stop MacGregor from butchering our industry.

The right to earn a living is a human right.

Is *this* policing?

The disgraceful scene above took place after the NEC meeting in Sheffield on April 12th. Seven policemen attacked one miner, putting the boot in, much to the satisfaction of the policeman on the right. Moments after this picture was taken by Rob Steerwood, police shoved the camera into his face.

John Tunney, a journalist on the Sheffield Morning Telegraph, independently confirmed the brutality. He wrote in his paper the following day: ". . . the police started pushing and shoving marchers in the back. Turning round seemed to be the cardinal offence and it was then that individuals were grabbed and thumped.

"Some were literally dragged away. Others had four or five policemen pinning them to the road. I did not see a single marcher strike a policeman, but I saw a number of marchers struck and manhandled."

181. The front page of a special (strike) issue of *The Miner*, published by the NUM on 16 April 1984. *NUM*

182. Photographer Martin Jenkinson superbly captures the unified mood of a mass rally of women's support groups – from all over the country – that assembled at the Civic Hall, Barnsley on 12 May 1984. *Martin Jenkinson*

183. The banner of the new Royston Drift Branch is prominent in a large demonstration through Mansfield, 14 May 1984. *D.J. Arkell/NUM*

184. The so-called 'Alamo' picket at Cortonwood (Brampton) captured the public imagination and generated much media interest. Here, the *Barnsley Chronicle* photographer was in attendance to record 'trimming' the Christmas tree.
Barnsley Chronicle

185. Terence Picken, seen here in 2000, proudly holding a Cortonwood commemorative plate, was a regular picket at the 'Alamo'. In very hard times, it was a place where he could get a decent meal, such was the generosity and support of local people.

186 & 187. Two historic photographs showing the NUM picket at Cortonwood, 25 January 1985.

Unlikely as it may seem, a *Daily Express* photographer gained the confidence of the regular pickets and took a unique view of the inside of the 'Alamo', complete with its 'modern conveniences'.

Terence Picken (wearing dark cap) had in fact just come out of hospital after being treated for pneumonia.

Daily Express/T.Picken

188. Picket duty at Barnsley area pits was normally both peaceful and good humoured but occasionally events became inflamed due to unnecessary actions. This appears to have been the case at Woolley Colliery on 30 October 1984, when branch secretary Ralph Summerfield was knocked to the ground and beaten on the head with truncheons. Ralph was simply talking to an inspector, appealing for the police to restrain dogs which, by their presence and deployment, had created a potentially violent confrontation. Ralph had to be conveyed to hospital for treatment.

189. This report appeared in the *Barnsley Chronicle* on 12 October 1984. It refers to the 'reappearance' of pawnbrokers in the town, a consequence of the hard times being experienced by mining families and communities.

Mining families' need for cash has prompted the reappearance of a pawnbrokers in Barnsley.

Thompson's, the Beech Street auctioneers, will accept "pledges" from next week.

"Mining families have been having to sell items to auctioneers or market traders because that's the only way they could raise money. Now they will be able to get short-term loans with the goods as security", said Mr. Cliff Thompson, a director of the family business.

Barnsley's last pawnbroker — The White House in Shambles Street — closed two years ago when it was thought there was no longer scope for such money-lending.

"We will obviously have to be very careful because of the amount of stolen property knocking about. We are working with the police on that and I would like

Striking families hit rock bottom

to get it across to the thieves, rogues and vagabonds that we're not a place for getting shut of bent gear", said Mr. Thompson.

The firm are now on the lookout for three brass balls — the traditional sign of the pawnbroker — to supplement the present painted sign designed by an art student.

A spokesman for the NCB said: "It's a sad reflection of the times that when the board are spending £450 million on pits in Barnsley a pawnbroker's shop has opened to cater for striking miners".

Barnsley councillors are considering making a plea to the Gov-

ernment for help to ease the spending crisis caused by the miners' dispute.

Barnsley Council now spend more than £35,000 a week on measures to combat suffering, and as the 30-week dispute drags on the financial burden is getting heavier.

This extra expenditure by the council on things like free school meals, free clothing, housing benefit and social services relief grants is still liable for penalty by the Government.

And six months into the financial year, the council will have their rate support grant cut next year by £3 million if existing spending levels are maintained.

Finance Committee chairman Coun. Bernard Goddard, said: "We are considering making some kind of plea to Environment Secretary Patrick Jenkin, that the money we have spent helping out during the miners' dispute be excluded from grant penalty".

TOGETHER

All out for victory

WE congratulate all of you who have stuck out for so long against all odds.

We recognise the hardship this has brought on you and your families — just as it has for miners and their families throughout the British coalfield.

This struggle has cost all too much hardship to turn back now. We appeal to every Yorkshire miner — stand together and we will win.

In Yorkshire Area only a handful of our men have returned to work. To those who have returned to work — we ask you to rejoin us.

No pit is safe — not any pit in the Yorkshire Area, no matter what coal reserves it has. Cortonwood has five years of good coal....

The union's only strength comes from standing together.

The board has tried to bribe you with what is already your money. You will get it whenever you go back.

Go back with the union — when we have won this great fight for jobs and a future!

Then you will go back with pride, with your head held high — and with the strength of your union to defend your interests in future.

TOGETHER WE WILL WIN!

JACK TAYLOR, president.
OWEN BRISCOE, general secretary.
KEN HOMER, financial secretary.
SAM THOMPSON, vice president.
And the NUM Yorkshire Area Executive.

Flashback to the first Special Delegate Conference of the strike, when it was little more than a month old. Thousands of Yorkshire miners lobbied delegates with a clear message — "The only way to end this struggle is by winning." After nine months of that struggle, the message is just the same. (Photo: Jacob Sutton)

WE WILL WIN!

190. 'Together We Will Win': despite over thirty weeks of hardship the Yorkshire NUM continued to be confident of 'victory' and going back to work only when pits and jobs were won. *NUM/The Miner*

191. Members of Barnsley Women Against Pit Closures receive money and food donated by the Greenham Common women. Yvonne Clapham receives cash from Fred Clowery, while Clive Hargreaves hands over food to Anne Thomes (centre) and Grace Burton.

192. Ralph Summerfield, NUM official at Woolley Colliery shakes hands with Ron Ralph of the Preston AEW, in appreciation of food donations during the strike. *Ralph Summerfield*

193-194　The Italian steelworkers' union sponsored thirty children of Woolley miners for a three week holiday (via KM Coaches), based at a small hotel in Angoloterme, northern Italy in January 1985. The children, now in their mid-twenties, had an unforgettable time, away from the misery of the strike. *Ralph Summerfield*

195. Pickets Graham Swayne (left) of Middlecliffe and Hedley Mitchell, from Wombwell at Dearne Valley Colliery, Little Houghton, in January 1985.

At the time it was reported that not one of the 400 men employed at the pit had returned to work. Dearne Valley was a small 'family pit' where fathers worked with sons, and brothers worked with cousins. NUM branch secretary Eric Mountain said it was 'unique in the way the men seem to stick together'.

The pit was sunk in 1897, becoming a surface drift mine six years later, serving the communities of Little Houghton, Middlecliffe and Great Houghton. Geological conditions made work difficult in the 1970s but the introduction of retreat mining restored profitability. Until the overtime ban, it was said that the pit produced 300,000 tonnes of coal p.a. with good bonuses paid. Eric Mountain felt convinced that Dearne Valley had a good future but also feared that the Coal Board could close it down at any moment.

Since the previous May, men from Dearne Valley were able to get a meal at Great Houghton Welfare Hall where sixteen women served up to 200 meals, five days each week, using just one electric cooker.

One picket summed up the mood: 'We want to go back when the time comes in a unified and dignified manner when the majority vote to go back and not as scabs.'

196. For some mining communities – in this case near Dearne's 'big brother pit' at Houghton Main – families lived under a situation resembling a military occupation. Here, a riot squad blocks the road in February 1985. Note the defiant stance of the women resident. *John Harris/NUM*

197. Striking miners digging for coal in old shallow workings between Shaw Lane Cricket Ground and Broadway, Barnsley.

198. (Right)
Cortonwood miners
refused to go back to
work when Kent
miners picketed their
pit at the end of the
strike. *John Harris.*

199. (Below)
This postcard was
produced to
commemorate the
'march back to work'
at Cortonwood on 5
March 1985. The
threat to close the pit
was generally
perceived as 'the
spark that started the
strike.' By October
the pit had closed.
Judson & Veasey

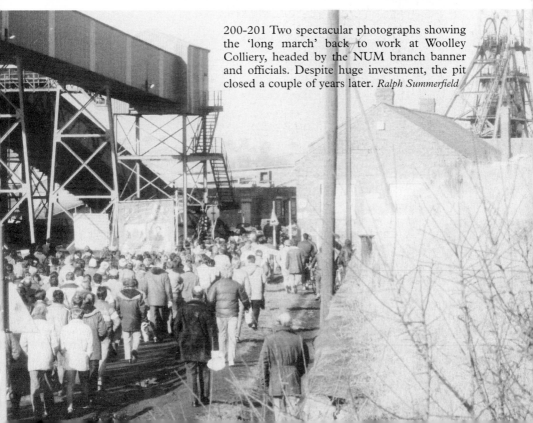

200-201 Two spectacular photographs showing the 'long march' back to work at Woolley Colliery, headed by the NUM branch banner and officials. Despite huge investment, the pit closed a couple of years later. *Ralph Summerfield*

202. The undue haste in which some pits were closed, buildings abandoned and sites obliterated from the local landscape is well illustrated by reference to Cortonwood Colliery. When local historian and former Rockingham miner Mr Arthur Clayton and myself made an unofficial visit to Cortonwood in April 1986, a few months after closure and a short time before the bulldozers arrived, it was a most eerie experience, with tools and equipment, even paperwork strewn everywhere. Graffiti on a workshop door just about summed up the feelings of the last miners. *Brian Elliott*

203. Arthur Clayton in Cortonwood pit yard, two silent headgears in the background. *Brian Elliott*

204-5. Headgear, Time and Wages Office, Cortonwood. *Brian Elliott*

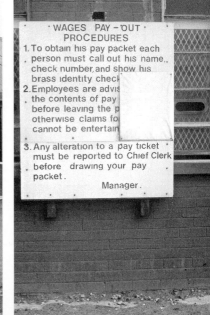

· WAGES PAY - 'OUT ·
PROCEDURES

1. To obtain his pay packet each
   person must call out his name,
   check number, and show his
   brass identity check

2. Employees are advis
   the contents of pay
   before leaving the p
   otherwise claims fo
   cannot be entertain

3. Any alteration to a pay ticket
   must be reported to Chief Clerk
   before drawing your pay
   packet.

                    Manager.

COAL BY THE MILE!

MINERS at Grimethorpe Colliery have just achieved their highest-ever tonnage for a single coalface.

They produced 17,338 tonnes in a week from C 64s, a 178-metres-long face in the Newhill seam. The previous best was 13,927 tonnes, set in March, 1982, on another Newhill face.

Productivity was an impressive 57 tonnes, the miners having travelled up and down the 6ft high face 92 times with their coal-cutting machine: a distance of 10.3 miles.

Total output for the week at the 1,350-man pit was 26,900 tonnes — the highest tonnage for 12 months.

206. Not long after the strike a number of Barnsley area pits were achieving remarkable production records. In this example, Grimethorpe miners celebrate '10.3 miles in 1 week' in March 1986, achieving a record 17,338 tonnes from the six-foot high Newhill face. *Barnsley Chronicle*

207. Machinery, miner – and sprags: the productive Newhill seam at Grimethorpe looks an impressive sight in this later (c.1991) photograph. *Johnny Wood*

Mining museum launched

A two million pound scheme to create a Yorkshire mining museum was launched at the 200-years-old Caphouse Colliery, between Huddersfield and Wakefield, last week.

The project, which involves South and West Yorkshire county councils, has been organised through the Yorkshire Mining Museum Trust Limited, a consortium of four local authorities and the NCB.

Caphouse Colliery, closed down in October of this year, still remains intact. The museum hopes to take advantage of the complete colliery to open it up to the public as a tourist attraction and to provide an opportunity for educational trips.

The museum, due to open late in 1986, will be developed in three stages: the first involves a guided underground tour; the second phase will open up more of the surface areas, while stage three is designed to fully exploit the site's general recreation potential.

Coal mining in the area around Caphouse dates from 1515, the colliery itself being shown on a plan of 1791, its pedigree well-established.

It is envisaged that the showpiece of the museum will be the workings 130 metres underground, more than 130,000 visitors being expected a year.

Chairman of the trust, County Coun. John Gunnell, leader of West Yorkshire County Council, who unveiled a commemorative plaque at the inauguration, said: "No area of this country has made a greater contribution to the history of mining and the energy wealth of this nation than South and West Yorkshire — the Yorkshire coalfield.

"It is therefore fitting that Yorkshire should have an exciting and imaginative project to recognise that contribution and that history.

"This resurrection of Caphouse as a working mining museum is such a project. I believe we are beginning today what will be a major national asset, sited here on the borders of West and South Yorkshire".

208. This report, taken from the *Barnsley Chronicle* of 13 December 1986, refers to the inauguration of the Caphouse Colliery, located between Wakefield and Huddersfield, as a new 'working mining museum', tourist and educational attraction. A key feature being underground guided tours. Like many other projects of this kind, annual visitor figures for the Yorkshire Mining Museum were over-optimistic but the museum thankfully survives – functioning since 1995 as a national institution and renamed The National Mining Museum for England.

209-210. My parents and family on a family visit to the Yorkshire Mining Museum, shortly after its opening. For many retired miners such as my father, the museum provided a great deal of interest, and also a unique opportunity for the wife and grandchildren to experience, for the first time, an underground visit to a real coal mine.

HOUGHTON DARFIELD
FASTEST MILLION

Something to smile about

987: SOMETHING to smile
bout: miners at Houghton/
Darfield Main, a year after the
its' merger, produced the
astest million tonnes of coal
n the Barnsley coalfield, two
months ahead of the previous

record held by Grimethorpe
(1981).

Despite huge gains in
productivity after the 1984/85
miners' strike and severe
cut-backs in manpower,
Barnsley pits were unable to
meet the stringent economic

guidelines laid down by British
Coal.

The privatisation of the
electricity generating industry
and the dash for gas in power
stations dealt the fatal blow to
the coalfield. British Coal.

211. 'Something to smile about' at Houghton/Darfield Main in 1987 when 'the
fastest million tonnes of coal in the Barnsley coalfield' was produced. *Barnsley
Chronicle*

OUGHTON Main NUM branch delegate Ken Hill with the delightful — but dam-
ed — banner.

'Help us restore banner'

HOUGHTON Main branch of the
National Union of Mineworkers
appealed for help this week to
restore their banner to its former glory.

Thirty seven years of regular
appearances at miners' demonstrations have taken their toll
and the 8' x 6' silk banner is
now tearing in the wind.

The branch, however, are
determined to restore rather
than replace the banner, which
has been described by one firm
capable of carrying out the
restoration work as "the best
we've seen".

First made around 1950, it con-
tains a large oil painting of Clem

Attlee, surrounded by a border of
silver flowers, with the words: "To
Prosperity" and "By Industry We
Flourish".

The reverse side bears a similar
oil painting of Sam Bullough, the
then president of the Yorkshire
area NUM with the words: "Health,
Safety and Welfare".

Mr. Tommy Delemere, NUM
branch secretary at Houghton
Main, told the Chronicle: "The same
firm which described the banner
as the best they'd seen also told
us it would cost around £500 to
restore. Unfortunately, we just
don't have that amount of money
available.

"We are looking at the possi-
bility of staging fund raising

events such as concerts and raffles,
but we also thought we should
appeal to the public at large.

"It could be that someone would
like to sponsor part of the restoration which is vitally necessary
because the actual silk is rotting
and tearing. The damage is mainly
at the bottom of the banner, but
also around the oil painting.

"I suppose it's also possible that
surviving relatives of Mr. Bullough
and Mr. Attlee might also like to
make a donation.

"We'd like to speak to anyone
who feels they can help us raise
the money. We are also on the
lookout for suitable premises
where the banner could be hung
when the restoration is complete.

212. Houghton Main NUM appeal for help to restore their banner which – on the
front – features a portrait of former Labour leader and PM Clement Atlee – and the
rear has the image of ex-Yorkshire Miners' President, Sam Bullough. *Barnsley
Chronicle, August 1987.*

213. Grimethorpe Colliery First Aid Team – shown here wearing their sponsored jumpers -were successful in winning the Wood Shield in 1987. Left to right, they are Jim Whitehead, John Howell, Ian Walker, Trevor Knight, Peter Kenworthy and Steven Gavin. *Ian Walker*

214. The Woolley NUM branch march along Eldon Street, Barnsley during the landmark 100th Yorkshire Miners' Gala and Demonstration, in 1987. The main speakers were Labour leader Neil Kinnock and NUM President Arthur Scargill.

215-216. Retired miner Robert 'Bob' Harper (b. Deepcar, 1900) as a young man and in his back garden at Barugh Green, aged 85.

I interviewed Bob when researching my family history in 1985. One of fourteen children from the marriage of Robert William and Mary Ellen Harper (nee Elliott), as a thirteen year old, Bob started work on the Parkgate screens at Dodworth, but after just a month moving on to 'tramming' underground where his father worked; and then went on to 'Stanhope' and 'Chemics' (Old Silkstone Collieries) pit in the Whinmoor seam. When this pit closed (March,1925) he moved to Woolley, continuing there until his retirement in 1965, having worked for 52 years as a coal miner. In his retirement, Bob was a very keen gardener and allotment holder, often successful with flowers and vegetables at village shows.

> **BARNSLEY METROPOLITAN BOROUGH COUNCIL**
>
> This memento marks the site of the former Beckett Hospital and Dispensary which was established on 14th March 1865. The original dispensary for outpatients was later extended to cope with increased numbers of injuries occurring in the expanding mining industry.
>
> The Hospital up-keep was financed from endowments, subscriptions and collections and more importantly, from Miners and Colliery Owners in the Barnsley Area.
>
> **1986**

217. Plaque attached to a stone memorial commemorating the former Barnsley Beckett Hospital and Dispensary which was extended in order to deal with mining accidents.

NORTH YORKS

ASKERN

Manager Ray Burdis

Askern, near Doncaster, was sunk in 1911 and is famous for some of the country's top quality house coal as well as producing power station fuel. Planned output this year from Warren House/Barnsley seam is 520,000 tonnes with a workforce of 470.

"This is the first full year that all our output will come from total retreat working, so we are looking for a productive 12 months. Our contribution, and bottom line, should improve when we move into the full Barnsley section in August with our heavy duty 63s retreat unit working in 2.54 metres. If we can get our cash flow right now and balance our books, the future looks very bright with a bonanza of thick coal to go at in the Pollington take. A full retreat system with high-speed haulages are planned as part of what would be almost a brand new pit".

BARNSLEY MAIN

Manager Colin Ives

Barnsley Main, Barnsley, was developed on the site of an old colliery in 1979. Along with Grimethorpe, Houghton Main and Dearne Valley, it helps make up the South Side complex where underground inter-colliery connections allow all the coal to be surfaced at Grimethorpe for treatment and dispatch at the South Side Coal Preparation Plant. Some 500 men work the Fenton and Parkgate seams with this year's output planned at 700,000 tonnes.

"Although our reserves are rapidly running out, we can make a positive contribution to the Group this year as we wind up our main developments and concentrate on production faces. They are short-life retreat units so our Dintheader drivages have to average a minimum of 60 metres a week if we are to avoid costly production gaps due to shortage of face room".

DEARNE VALLEY

Manager Ray Wiles

Dearne Valley, Little Houghton, near Barnsley, is a drift mine which began working the Shafton seam in 1903. A vertical borehole connects to Grimethorpe's coal clearance system for treatment at South Side. Planned output of 355,000 tonnes from Sharlston Yard seam with 255 men. The pit supplies the local Coalite works as well as power station market.

"Working the Group's thinnest coal, varying from 70 to 85cm, means we have to run very hard to stand still. But if we continue to perform as we did in the speedy transfer of equipment from BY14s 'dog leg' and the setting-off of BY14s face, we have every chance of making Dearne Valley a viable concern. We now have to do our own salvage and installation – and with only one retreat face in operation, we have to prove we can do it better and faster than anyone else. I would like to thank all our workforce for the first class co-operation we have enjoyed in recent months. If that team spirit continues, we will finish the financial year in the black."

DENBY GRANGE

Manager John Blundell

Denby Grange, Netherton, near Wakefield, is Yorkshire's oldest pit which can trace its roots back to 1791. Some 450 men work the Whinmoor and Beeston seams. All the coal is surfaced via an underground connection at the West Side Coal Preparation Plant at Woolley, mainly for the power station market.

"We have got problems with a middle dirt band that has thickened to 0.8m and we do become vulnerable when we are down to one face. The geology in Hartley Bank area is uncertain and we have lost some face room due to a thick dirt band that is more extensive than we first thought. At the other side of the pit, there is also a thickening dirt band in 46s area and the coal at the Calder end is only a metre thick. This situation, along with a very low vend and high infrastructure costs, is why the pit is under review at the present time."

218. A brochure produced by British Coal's (slimmer) North Yorkshire Group – based at Allerton Bywater – included brief details of its 11 collieries. The three not illustrated here are Kellingley, Prince of Wales (Pontefract) and Sharlston (nr Wakefield). In the introduction Group Director Bob Siddall wrote in confident terms about making the new Group 'No.1' in Britain, most of the pits being 'in good shape physically' and 'with almost 100% of our bulk output now coming from retreat mining' pits were said to be on course for achieving record tonnages. *British Coal*

FRICKLEY

Manager Malcolm High

Frickley, South Elmsall, near Pontefract, is one of six million-tonnes-a-year pits in the Group. Sunk in 1903, a £28m investment scheme to access the Newhill and Meltonfield seams was recently completed and development work has just started. Annual output from Top Haigh Moor and Cudworth seams is planned at 1,050,000 tonnes with 830 men. Pit supplies power station and industrial markets including Courtaulds, British Tissues and Smurfitt Paper.

"I have only been here a short time but one thing is already obvious – we have the potential this year to achieve the best results in Frickley's history. We have three retreat faces for nearly the whole of the year on seven machine shifts – with one of our new installations, L29s, capable of filling the shaft on its own. One or two of our faces have already achieved 90 per cent of potential some weeks, and we now have two new sets of heavy duty 4x500 tonne forward walkway shield supports purpose-designed for inter-action problems. If we put past industrial relations problems behind us and work together as a team, we are set for an excellent run at around £1 a gigajoule. That's good news for Frickley, the men who work here and the village of South Elmsall as well as North Yorkshire Group".

GOLDTHORPE

Manager Arthur Hendy

Goldthorpe, near Barnsley, is one of the jewels in British Coal's crown. This 80-year-old drift mine continues to produce some of Britain's cheapest coal – consistently undercutting foreign fuel prices. One of the country's most profitable pits, it regularly operates at £1 a gigajoule or less despite low proceeds. Planned output this year is 850,000 tonnes from the Shafton seam with a workforce of 513 – all its coal going to power stations.

"We have had a tremendous last 12 months with a record ouput of 1.177m tonnes and a substantial profit. And there's more to come now our first two heavy duty retreat faces are on stream. At a cost of £5 million , these units represent our biggest-ever investment and we'll be looking to better last year's overall output a manshift of nine tonnes. It isn't easy coal here – the Shafton is dirty, our short-life faces only take a 1.5m section and we suffer from poor roof conditions. But come July, we will start to realise the full potential of Goldthorpe with two long faces working in tandem for the first time. We shall then start to perform at optimum levels.".

GRIMETHORPE

Manager David Brook

Grimethorpe, near Barnsley, sunk in 1894, is the hub of the South Side scheme. All output from the complex is brought to the surface at Grimethorpe via a 2,650m long 1-in-4 drift on two 48-inch wide computer-controlled conveyor belts. The No. 1 lower measures conveyor is driven by a 6,000 h.p. motor, has a top running speed of 300 metres a minute and can clear coal at the rate of up to 2,000 tonnes an hour. It is then transported by overland conveyor to the South Side washery for treatment and dispatch. Another of the Group's million-tonners working the Fenton, Parkgate and Newhill seams with a workforce of 900. Grimethorpe supplies a wide range of markets including domestic, industrial, coking, export and electricity generation.

"We have made a good recovery since the fire in Fenton seam last September, and the pit is now set up for a profitable year. Parkgate T22s is performing very well in a 2.4m section, and we have T35s face line opened up now as replacement. In Fenton, we are now equipping the replacement face for Rits which doesn't finish until July, so this will be available as a spare unit from the end of May. Our first face in the newly-developed North Fenton area – due to come on stream next March – is already headed out and looks a very promising prospect indeed. Another big plus for Grimethorpe will come in three months time when we will have a spare face to cover breakdowns and poor geology. There is no reason why we shouldn't achieve our planned output of 1m tonnes as well as developing enough face room for the following year. That's the big difference and the key factor in transforming Grimethorpe's fortunes – the men are now very aware that today's development is tomorrow's coal.".

HOUGHTON MAIN

Manager David Walton

Houghton Main, Little Houghton, near Barnsley, was sunk in 1873 and is another million-tonner feeding into the South Side Coal Preparation Plant via an underground connection to Grimethorpe. It merged with neighbouring Darfield in November, 1986. Output from Fenton and Silkstone seams is planned at 1.1m tonnes this year with 900 men.

"The pit looks sound with four faces working most of the year and a fifth coming on stream in November. I am confident we will achieve our output target and finish the year in the black. After a fair degree of success with our first retreat face in the Silkstone, we are now planning a second. We also pioneered Yorkshire's first all-electric shearer, the Anderson Strathclyde Electra, which has been a real winner for us – producing almost half of last year's output of nearly 1m tonnes. Our fourth Electra face in the Fenton, 36s, comes into production in November and will give us a big boost in the latter part of the year. Development performance is also picking up and we have been achieving 80 per cent of planned rates in recent months which will stand us in good stead for the future.".

219. The South Side Coal Preparation Plant at Grimethorpe Colliery is described as "the biggest and most high-tech in Europe" by manager Barry Todd in the 1990 British Coal brochure. *British Coal*

220. Houghton Main had the benefit of Yorkshire's 'first all-electric shearer' – the Anderson Strathclyde Electra – which had produced almost half of the pit's output of nearly 1m tonnes in 1989. *British Coal*

221. A most impressive view of a modern shearer at work on the face at Goldthorpe Colliery, a successful drift mine which, in 1990, was said to be 'where some of Britain's cheapest coal is produced.' Principally working the Shafton seam, it remained in production for just four more years, the last 'Barnsley' pit to close. *British Coal*

Fury as 30,00

Stephen Walsh

BRITAIN's coal industry was brought to its knees last night with the crushing announcement that 31 pits are to cease production with the loss of 30,000 jobs — almost a third of them in Yorkshire.

The size of the cuts, which will leave just 19 working mines and slash coal production by almost two-thirds, exceeded the worst fears of the pit communities and was immediately attacked by stunned miners' leaders.

British Coal's much-leaked confirmation of the swingeing closures — to begin this week — started a political storm last night.

Board of Trade President Michael Heseltine immediately announced a £1bn package to meet redundancy payments and help devastated mining areas — but it was roundly denounced by the local authority-backed Coalfield Communities Campaign as insufficient.

Labour described the closures as "vandalism of our energy resources", adding: "The rest of Europe must think we are mad to abandon such a rich asset."

Meanwhile miners' leader Arthur Scargill said mineworkers would be urged to take "whatever industrial action" necessary to defend pits.

The closure programme — to begin with six pits on Friday — was blamed on the reduced demand for coal from the privatised power industry, but opponents claimed the motive was more political than economic.

British Coal said it would reduce output by at least 25m tonnes per year by closing 27 collieries and mothballing another four, leaving just 19 working mines.

The pits on the "hit list" include eight to close and three to be mothballed in Yorkshire with the loss of 8,678 jobs. The cuts will mean the end of deep mining in North Derbyshire, Lancashire, North Staffordshire, and North Wales.

British Coal's chairman, Neil Clarke, making the grim announcement in London, conceded the closure of so many mines and loss of jobs would be "grievous".

He added: "Everything possible must be done to ease the difficulties which will be faced by those leaving British Coal, by their families and their communities."

The National Union of Mineworkers' president, Arthur Scargill, urged his men to stand and fight "the most savage, brutal, act of vandalism in modern times".

He said: "This has got nothing to do with economics.

"It cannot be justified on social grounds. It is a deliberate political act of industrial vandalism perpetrated against an already decimated industrial landscape."

The NUM executive meets in London today ahead of a special delegate conference of miners' officials in Sheffield tomorrow at which the union's Yorkshire area will call for members to be balloted on industrial action.

The vice-president of the Yorkshire NUM, Ken Capstick, said: "We don't know if we will succeed. But after this announcement, I cannot see that people in those pits have anything to lose."

British Coal is hoping to head off any strikes with improved pay-offs of up to

£37,000 for redu workers, while warn any industrial acti mean severe cuts i payments.

Employee Rel Director Kevan Hu the harsh realities closure programme miners were being o "one-way ticket" ou

"Disruptive ind action will result withdrawal of all e payments for involved," he warn

Generators have lion tonnes of coal and British Coal is st million tonnes at co enough spare fuel a year.

Neil Greatrex, No dent of the brea Union of Demo Miners, urged the take action to pro jobs of miners and in other industries.

The chairman of th shire group of Labo Kevin Barron, the for Rother Valle demned the closures biggest act of vanda the history of Br industrial life".

The Bishop of S Rt Rev David Lur condemned the dec

miners sacked

ield communities as
ess" and a wicked
of God-given
es.
Heseltine said the
ackage was being
available for redun-
pay-offs and to help
ate closure areas.
escribed approving
losses as "the tough-
sion I have ever had
e".

sh Coal chairman
rke said: "It is a very
for British Coal, for
s employees, myself
colleagues.
ever much we dis-
, and we dislike this
rongly...it is a reality
hich we are going to
live."

cale and speed of the
undown shocked
politicians and com-
leaders even though
ad been braced for
e closures.
leave the country's
ing 11,000 miners
g amid the ruins of
istry that employed
miners at 958 col-
when it was national-
1947.
ire yesterday's
ncement, 41,000
were working at 50

222-223. This headline and report appeared on the front
page of the *Yorkshire Post* on Wednesday 14 October
1992, the day after British Coal Chairman's Neil
Clarke's horrendous pit closure announcement in
London, described by NUM President, Arthur Scargill
as 'the most savage, brutal, act of vandalism in modern
times'.

224. 'SACK MAJOR NOT THE MINERS':
Grimethorpe miners assemble at Churchfields prior to a
protest march against pit closures (also see image
number 231). *Johnny Wood*

MINING MA

THE DECISION to nail down the coffin lid
on the once thriving Barnsley coalfield has
been slammed from every quarter of the
local community and beyond.

The coalfield, which boasted more than 30 pits
employing 46 per cent of the town's total workforce in
1961, has gradually declined in recent times leaving
just two in the area — Grimethorpe and Houghton
Main employing 1,300.

The latest proposals to close 31 pits nationally, including the two Barnsley pits by October 30, stunned
unions, politicians, community and church leaders
alike with its scale and speed.

The closure programme — with the first six pits
closing today (Friday) — was blamed on a reduced
demand for coal from the privatised power industry,
but opponents claim the motive to shed 30,000 jobs
was more political than economical.

But there was good news for Goldthorpe pit, which
is to continue production. Goldthorpe, which was not
part of the old Barnsley coalfield, was included in the
"hit list" leaked two weeks ago.

"This has got nothing to do with economics," said
miners' president Arthur Scargill, commenting on the
closures. He described the decision as revenge for the
1984 coal strike.

"It cannot be justified on social grounds ... it is a
deliberate political act of industrial vandalism perpetrated against an already decimated industrial landscape," he said.

Eric Illsey, MP for Barnsley Central, has written
to Prime Minister John Major requesting a meeting
and Barnsley Council leader Hedley Salt reacted with
"bitter disappointment" at the announcement saying:

"My heart goes out to the families and communities
that are affected by the tragic news. Barnsley Council
will continue to fight against these closures."

In a joint Press statement Michael Clapham, MP for
Barnsley West and Penistone and an ex-Dodworth
Colliery miner, and Mr. Illsley, said details of the closures had been deliberately leaked to prepare for the
official announcement but "the callous and brutal way
in which British Coal have acted has disgusted the
British public".

Richard Davies, Director of the council's Economic
Development Department is equally concerned with
the knock-on effect that the area's economy will suffer
as a result of the proposed closures.

"The proposed closures will obviously have conse-
quences not just for the miners but for the shop-
keepers, garages and all the other services that are
purchased locally — once again Barnsley is going to
suffer," he said.

Miners will receive up to £37,000 in redundancy pay
— although managers have warned that any industrial action taken against the closures will severely
jeopardise those payments.

This threat is not been taken idly by the men at
Grimethorpe and Houghton Main as Albert Clarke,
who, like many of the last men at Grimethorpe was

THE high noon of the coal industry: miners at Woolley Colliery in
town reinforced its reputation as the coal centre of South Yorksh
however, Doncaster had become the coal capital.

SSACRE

born and bred in the village, said:

"I was on strike in 1984 and would not have gone back. But this time a strike will not save our jobs."

Leader of Brierley Town Council, Coun. Alex Vodden said the announcement was "disastrous" for the Grimethorpe community and added: "Redundancy payments do not compensate for people's futures as no amount of money can provide the confidence a person gets from his ability to look after himself and his kids by his own efforts."

The Bishop of Sheffield, who described the announcement as "sheer madness" was joined in his criticism by the Rector of Darfield, Rev. Martin Brown.

Mr. Brown said that, although he is far removed politically from Arthur Scargill, the miners' president was right in saying that decimation of the mining industry is pure vandalism.

Mr. Brown, in whose parish live many of people who will be put out of work, said that the Government has made a "complete kack-handed mess" by privatising energy without introducing regulations about the supply it uses and in subsidising something that will not last, because, he claims, nuclear power will be too expensive.

"There is no social reason, no economic reason, nor any political reason that can be seen for the decision," he said. "There is a lot of bellyaching about markets, but the reason markets do not want coal is because the Government have subsidised nuclear power — which is 300 per cent more expensive.'

Wombwell hospital consultant and Labour Party member Sharad Mahatme described the decision as lunacy and claims that unless it is reversed the Labour Party should withdraw its support for the Maastricht Treaty.

"Now is the time for John Smith not only to support and win the hearts of 30,000 miners and their families, but also millions of others who cannot understand the lunacy of closing pits at this time."

The Barnsley-based Coalfield Communities Campaign's Parliamentary Officer Andrew Freeman called on the Government to reverse their decision saying: "After all the pain Barnsley has been through as a result of the wave of pit closures in the 1980s, it is bad that the town is going to have to suffer again.

"But I am convinced that Barnsley will bounce back; Barnsley Council have one of the best records in the country for going out and looking for jobs to replace the ones that have been lost.

"As well as that process continuing, it is going to need the Government to come to the aid of Barnsley and other coal communities."

Willowgarth High School, Grimethorpe, is to play its part in the fight against pit closures by helping the community to put over its views to the general public.

With the help of the Yorkshire Arts Circus, the teachers are to produce a book on the pit which will be published before the colliery closes.

1900 and 1914 the
20s and early 30s,

Teachers are to give up the first day of their half-term holiday to interview members of the community on their mining recollections, the history of the pit, the closure and on the future of the village.

225. By copy deadline of Thursday 15 October, journalists at the *Barnsley Chronicle* had worked remarkably fast, producing an 'End of an Era' two-page special report on the pit closure announcement.

The front page headline 'Mining Massacre' and accompanying report included quotes from local MP's, Council leaders, clerics, miners and a representative from the Coalfields Communities Campaign.

The front page editorial piece described the Government's handling of the latest pit closures as 'political suicide', bemoaning the great waste of government money on recent colliery redevelopments, though, finishing optimistically, 'the strength and character of its [Barnsley's] folk will again help it over yet another hurdle of life.'

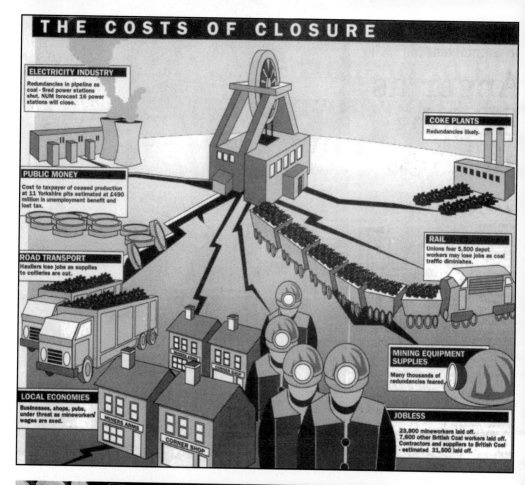

THE COSTS OF CLOSURE

ELECTRICITY INDUSTRY
Redundancies in pipeline as coal - fired power stations shut. NUM forecast 16 power stations will close.

COKE PLANTS
Redundancies likely.

PUBLIC MONEY
Cost to taxpayer of ceased production at 11 Yorkshire pits estimated at £490 million in unemployment benefit and lost tax.

ROAD TRANSPORT
Hauliers lose jobs as supplies to collieries are cut.

RAIL
Unions fear 5,500 depot workers may lose jobs as coal traffic diminishes.

LOCAL ECONOMIES
Businesses, shops, pubs, under threat as mineworkers' wages are axed.

MINING EQUIPMENT SUPPLIES
Many thousands of redundancies feared.

JOBLESS
23,800 mineworkers laid off. 7,600 other British Coal workers laid off. Contractors and suppliers to British Coal - estimated 31,500 laid off.

MINERS ARMS

CORNER SHOP

226. From major industries to corner shops, this graphic serves as a very good representation of the enormous economic and social impact of pit closures. *Yorkshire Post*

227. For younger miners in areas like Grimethorpe, with families and mortgages, it meant many attempts to seek alternative work or retraining via the Job Shop/British

228. This report by Andrew Glyn of Oxford University, commissioned by the NUM, outlined in considerable detail the economic case against pit closures, including the wider social effects not captured in financial calculations. So-called 'unprofitable' or 'uneconomic' pits should not be labelled as such because of their wider social importance. The government would be worse off due to lost tax revenues (from pay) and having to pay benefits, in fact, the report concluded: 'there are no pits whatsoever whose closure would benefit Government revenue.' *NUM*

The Economic Case Against Pit Closures

Prepared for the National Union of Mineworkers
by Andrew Glyn
Fellow and Tutor in Economics
Corpus Christi College, Oxford
And Associate Member Oxford University
Institute of Economics and Statistics

229. The future of Grimethorpe's famous brass band, seen here in practice, was also said to be in question. The band, 'Grimley' and the strike was to be the context of the highly acclaimed film *Brassed Off!*, with Pete Postlethwaite giving a memorable performance as the veteran conductor. The award-winning band gained the sponsorship of a private company: RJB Mining of Harworth. *Johnny Wood*

United we stand: Miners and their supporters pour through Barnsley as people power takes on Government over pit closures. Picture: Christine Boyd

Disaster warning to local economy

CLOSURE of pits in the Barnsley area will cost businesses and services more than £50m.

That was the warning from the Labour leader of Barnsley council, Hedley Salt, at a weekend rally in the town.

Coun Salt said council officers had calculated the losses to the local economy from a knock-on effect of the colliery job losses.

He urged the people of Barnsley to take to the streets to show their anger at British Coal's Government-backed plan for the nation's pits.

The rally followed a march through the town by more than 3,000 protesters led by the union banners of Grimethorpe and Houghton Main collieries, two of the pits where coal-cutting was stopped by BC on Friday.

Traffic ground to a halt as the march wound its way through the town.

Shoppers lined the streets to applaud the demonstrators, and shop assistants left their counters to come out and cheer.

Grimethorpe union branch secretary Ken Hancock challenged Board of Trade President Michael Heseltine to visit Grimethorpe and Houghton Main.

He told the rally: "We challenge him and the rest of his Tory colleagues to come to these pits and we will show them they are profitable.

"I dare them to come to Barnsley and risk being proved wrong."

Barnsley Central MP Eric Illsley, one of three MPs to speak, warned that dependency on gas at the expense of coal was foolhardy.

He said: "Never believe the Government's lie about a 90-day consultation period over the pits or that there will be a long-term review.

"They will bring coal in from Colombia, South Africa, and Australia and in four years the gas will have gone and will then be brought in from Norway and Russia."

Paul Jegger, of Yorkshire and Humberside TUC, cautioned: "The redundancy payments are simply advance payments in social security.

"If people believe they are going to take the money and set up business in something like computer software they'd better think again. The Government knows there are going to be no jobs."

Barnsley West MP Terry Patchett: "The country should apologise to Arthur Scargill for disbelieving him when he warned what would happen to our pits."

An even bigger demonstration is expected in Barnsley next Saturday, when Mr Scargill leads another march through the town.

230. Barnsley miners, their families and supporters took to the streets on 31 October 1992, in protest of pit closures, reported in some detail by the *Yorkshire Post*.

231. A crowd of about 5,000 packed into Barnsley town centre a week later (7 November 1992) in a Fight For Coal Rally in protest at the Government-sponsored pit closure programme.

Speakers included NUM President, Arthur Scargill and the Right Reverend Nigel McCulloch, Bishop of Wakefield. Ukrainian cosmonaut Alexander Volkov, on a goodwill visit from Gorlovka, joined in the protest. *Wes Hobson/Barnsley Chronicle*

232. A close-up photograph of a boy with a 'Save Our Pits' sticker attached to his forehead was a symbolic protest on behalf of the next generation. *Wes Hobson/Barnsley Chronicle*

233. A minor's message: eleven year old Matthew Hancock from Grimethorpe with the banner he carried during a protest march through London on Wednesday 21 October 1992. Matthew's father, Ken Hancock, was branch secretary at Grimethorpe. *Jim Moran*

ENERGY IS COAL

GRIMETHORPE

PIT CLOSURES

234. Mel Dyke, deputy head at Willowgarth School responded to the pit closure announcement by contacting Brian Lewis of Yorkshire Arts Circus and the writer Stan Barstow, author of *A Kind of Loving*, in order to discuss some kind of project to celebrate almost a century of coal mining at Grimethorpe Colliery. The result was 'a book-in-a-day', compiled on Saturday 24 October 1992, and published a few days later. It was produced by local children, their parents and grandparents with guidance from volunteer professional writers, poets, artists and teachers. There were also messages of support and encouragement from many well-known local and national personalities. *Mel Dyke/Yorkshire Arts Circus*

The book, *Energy is Coal* was an instant success, capturing the public imagination and generating much media attention, including the BBC *Everyman* programme; but more importantly, it was an opportunity for people of all ages and backgrounds to express their feelings about pit closures, and celebrate their mining heritage.

One of the oldest contributors was seventy-nine year old Maggie Harper whose grandfather, Daniel Hughes, had helped to sink the pit. Her father, Thomas Hughes, was one of the first 'Grimey' pony drivers and her late husband George had worked at Grimethorpe and Houghton Main for a total of 51 years. 'This book is supposed to make them think again about shutting the pit', said angry Maggie to *The Star* reporter, '-but they've nowt to think with.'

Humour was used to make a point, among the many moving contributions:

'Thy're opening a new factory in Cudworth and it's going to employ 32,000 redundant miners.'

'Give over Jim, what's it going to make?'

'Mothballs! Eighteen thousand mothballs per hour, and we're going to take them to all the pits in Yorkshire as well as Nottingham [shire] and shovel them down the shaft. Then when all the pits have been mothballed, they're going to wait fifteen years and then they're going to want men to shovel the balls back out again.' *Mel Dyke/Yorkshire Arts Circus*

The Prime Minister
10, Downing Street
London,

Dear Mr Major;
                    I am ashamed of a fellow Chelsea
F.C. Supporter, That Supporter is you. I thought
myself that you would be the right person for
the Prime Minister job, but I have changed my
mind. Everybody is disapointed at your decison about
Grimethorpe, especially the miners and their families.
My friends Brother John works at the coalite, John
is disgusted at your actions and so are other
people who are employed by coalite. I ask you
would you shut the pits if your family worked
or lived in grimethorpe. I hope when you see
the thousands of letters against the closures
you see sense, the sense is to think of
the people and keep the pits open.

                    Yours Sincerely,
                    Simon Lindley aged 12

235-236.
Schoolchildren from Willowgarth expressed their feelings by writing to the Prime Minister. Here is a typical example, from twelve-year old Simon Lindley - and the disappointing and, as it turned out, the only impersonal reply, received a month later.

Scottish miners, on a march from Glasgow to London, diverted to Willowgarth in recognition of the school and community's efforts. One pupil, Graham Bradbury, aged twelve, in a wonderful piece of creative writing, described the 'magic in the air' as the miners were given a tumultous welcome, several of them moved to tears.

10 DOWNING STREET
LONDON SW1A 2AA

From the Correspondence Secretary 30 November 1992

Dear Children,

       The Prime Minister has asked me to thank you for your recent letters which are receiving attention. A reply will be sent to you as soon as possible.

                    Yours sincerely,
                    Frances See

The Children
Willowgarth High School
Brierley Road
Grimethorpe
BARNSLEY
S72 8AJ

237-238. On Thursday 17 December 1992, Willowgarth School (and representatives from other mining community schools) were invited to Westminster Abbey for the Coalfields' Communities Campaign Christmas Carol Service. Here some of the Willowgarth pupils (there were over 600 from Willowgarth in attendance) can be seen in the Abbey and with the Bishop of Wakefield, Nigel McCulloch, outside 10 Downing Street where they handed in protest letters. *Mel Dyke*

239-241. 2 February 1993, was the day when a copy of *Energy is Coal* was handed in to 10 Downing Street by two pupil representatives: Claire Geeson (age 12) and Sally Middleton (16). In attendance and shown on the lower photograph were actress Alison Steadman and (with deputy head Mel Dyke) shadow Education Secretary Anne Taylor MP. *Mel Dyke*

242. (Below) The Mayor of Barnsley, Eric Illsley MP and dignitaries escort leader Neil Kinnock on a visit to Willowgarth School during the so-called 90 day pit review period. The Opposition Leader paid tribute to the pupils and staff who had done so much to bring to the world's attention the plight of coalfield communities such as Grimethorpe. *Mel Dyke*

243. Three women in a hot air balloon ascend from the Women Against Pit Closures camp at Houghton Main Colliery on 4 March 1993, just before the NUM/NACODS/RMT (Rail union) ballots for industrial action. A total of 21,424 of NUM members (60% of total membership) voted 'Yes'. *Women's Support Cards/Dave Douglass*

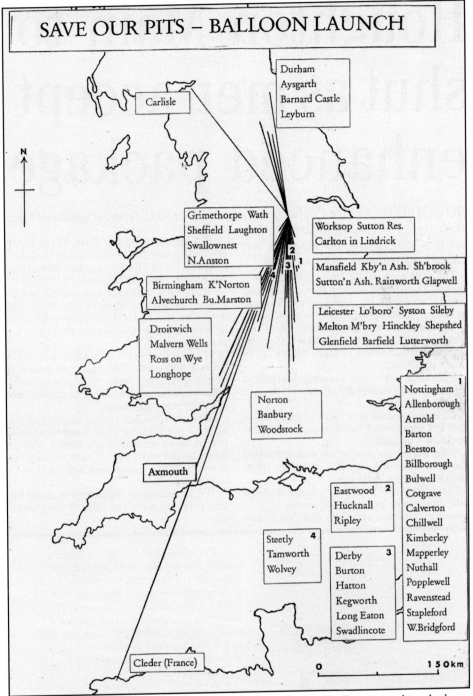

SAVE OUR PITS – BALLOON LAUNCH

Durham
Aysgarth
Barnard Castle
Leyburn

Carlisle

Grimethorpe Wath
Sheffield Laughton
Swallownest
N.Anston

Worksop Sutton Res.
Carlton in Lindrick

Mansfield Kby'n Ash. Sh'brook
Sutton'n Ash. Rainworth Glapwell

Birmingham K'Norton
Alvechurch Bu.Marston

Leicester Lo'boro' Syston Sileby
Melton M'bry Hinckley Shepshed
Glenfield Barfield Lutterworth

Droitwich
Malvern Wells
Ross on Wye
Longhope

Norton
Banbury
Woodstock

Nottingham   1
Allenborough
Arnold
Barton
Beeston
Billborough
Bulwell
Cotgrave
Calverton
Chillwell
Kimberley
Mapperley
Nuthall
Popplewell
Ravenstead
Stapleford
W.Bridgford

Axmouth

Eastwood   2
Hucknall
Ripley

Steetly   4
Tamworth
Wolvey

Derby   3
Burton
Hatton
Kegworth
Long Eaton
Swadlincote

Cleder (France)

0   150km

244. Shortly after the hot air ascent, smaller 'Save Our Pits' balloons were launched by Willowgarth High School children. As can be seen by the map, the balloons were found at diverse locations, and messages of support included several from individuals with mining associations, a doctor on his rounds, a primary school class on a field study course, a 'muck-spreading' farmer, workers at East Midlands Airport, Repton High School, the Earl of Lanesborough (Kegworth) and François Grall, a farmer in an artichoke field at Kernevez Cleder, Brittany! *Mel Dyke*

Houghton Main to shut as men accept enhanced package

HOUGHTON MAIN Colliery will shut today (Friday) following the men's decision to accept an enhanced redundancy package.

The 220 men made their decision at a packed Darfield Working Men's Club yesterday when they voted overwhelmingly in favour of accepting the new package.

The package will mean that 200 of the 220 men will be better off than under the previous redundancy terms — some by as much as £8,000.

Speaking after the meeting Houghton Main's branch secretary, Barry Hyde said he was devastated.

"The men asked us to make enquiries to find out what was available under the new package," he said.

"We made the enquiries and informed the men what was on offer and they voted to take the new package.

"In effect the men have been starved out; they have reduced the men's income over a long period and then dangled a carrot — it's nothing short of industrial blackmail."

The MP for Barnsley East, Terry Patchett — a former NUM delegate at Houghton Main — said the enhanced redundancy payments were outrageous.

"If the Government's arguments for closure of the pit are so good why don't they wait for the review to fully take place rather than use tax payers money to buy the miners out."

Meanwhile at Grimethorpe, NUM branch secretary Ken Hancock said that at present there were no plans to hold a branch meeting on whether or not to accept the enhanced payments.

"British Coal are trying to put the men against the branch. They have tried wearing us down and have gradually whittled down to the hard-core of lads — now they are dangling a carrot and hoping that the lads accept it.

"I'll be telling my members to stand firm and carry on with the fight if they want a job."

245. The closure of Houghton Main as reported in the *Barnsley Chronicle*, 30 April 1993. The strategy of British Coal to offer 'enhanced packages' obviated the need for a colliery review process. The latter was theoretically available but practically impossible given this approach; and it also resulted in some antipathy between union members and the branch.
Barnsley Chronicle

246. The modern looking No.2 tower winder at Houghton Main photographed by Colin Massingham, 27 January 1982.

247-249. Demolition and salvage work began at Houghton Main in 1994. A London-based protest group had unsuccessfully applied to English Heritage in the summer of 1993 to have the colliery buildings 'listed' as of historic or architectural interest. There were further protests from local people in October 1993 when British Coal announced its intention to demolish the former pit buildings at both Houghton and Grimethorpe, even before proper safety and conservation checks had been carried out. Veteran campaigner May O'Brien said that the loss of Houghton would lead to a loss of a vital part of Barnsley's heritage. Ken Hancock referred to the Grimethorpe decision as 'disgraceful', adding that 'it was probably the worst news that I have heard in twenty years.' *Johnny Wood*

Defiant miners fail to save pit from closure

THE day which the last few miners at Grimethorpe Colliery had been dreading since last October finally arrived on Friday when the last shifts went down. Fifteen men turned up for the day shift and four men and five officials went down at 12 noon on the last 'afters' shift. Over the last few months the workforce had dwindled as more and more of the 959 miners at the colliery on that fateful day in October took enhanced redundancy payments and left the industry. Only a few hardliners had optimistically hung on, hoping for a last-minute reprieve.

On Friday many of them just could not believe it had actually happened. For most of them it was a day of nostalgia and sentimentality.

Johnny Wood, once a faceworker at the pit where he had worked since he left school 18 years ago, could not resist slotting his timecard into its old position on the Parkgate Seam board where it had been placed on so many occasions over the years.

"I feel as though somebody is telling me I have to turn a life support machine off, as I class all the lads as my family," he said. "We have always looked after one another."

Johnny was born in Grimethorpe and has been on the NUM Committee at the colliery for the last three years. And what of his future? "I will be unemployed; what other job can I get? I have considered various things but intend to find a course in further education," he said.

Johnny considers himself a lot luckier than some as he is married but has no children, and no mortgage.

Three of the last men to go down on Friday were Michael Steel of Cudworth, Mark Webster of Royston and Neil Sykes of Barnsley. "I am really sickened and sluffened," said Mark. "We have been backed into a corner."

Neil dramatically compared the day to the Holocaust. "I imagine the Jews must have felt like this when they were digging their own graves," he said.

The feeling was echoed through the village, where the colliery has been its life-blood. Coun. Arthur Whittaker said: "I am absolutely shocked that it has come to closure. When we say we come from Grimethorpe, we describe it as a little mining village, but what now....?"

by GILLIAN PICKER

There has been speculation that Grimethorpe Colliery could be sold. If that does happen it will not attract Ken Hancock. "I shall certainly not work in the industry under privatisation," he said. "The terms and conditions are not the same and the accident record is deplorable."

The Women Against Pit Closures intend to stay at their camp outside the colliery indefinitely. "If they feel they can achieve something, good luck to them," said Ken, "but it is too late to save Grimethorpe."

The Coalfield Communities Campaign has striven to save the local collieries at a cost of over £100,000 to Barnsley Council. "I do not think the campaign has been in vain," said Coun. Whittaker. "We have put up a fight."

Chairman of the campaign, Coun. Hedley Salt said: "It would be criminal to stop now. If there is a market for coal then there is a good case for keeping Grimethorpe open. There are 50/60 years of readily available coal in the colliery; it is an almost priceless national asset."

There is to be a march on Friday morning as a final act to commemorate the deaths of the men who died working at the colliery in the last 98 years. It will leave Grimethorpe WMC at 11am and a wreath will be laid at the colliery.

The future of the colliery band has not yet been decided. "The lads are keen to carry on," said band secretary Ken Hirst, "but a lot depends on finance."

250. The last day at Grimethorpe... as reported in the *Barnsley Chronicle* (14 May 1993) by Gillian Picker.

251. Johnny Wood places his card in the old place on the Parkgate Seam time-card board for the last time. Three of the last miners to work were Mark Webster of Cudworth, Michael David Steel of Royston and Neil Sykes of Barnsley.

252. A group of key workers were involved with maintenance, salvage work, shaft filling etc. during 1993-94. Number 2 shaft 'Chair' going down the last time, 18 February 1994. *Ian Walker*

253. An impromptu notice of the 'Last Draw from Parkgate'. On-setter's cabin. *Ian Walker*

254-255. Once the 'chair' had gone, access was via a make-shift kibble, lowered down the shaft. *Ian Walker*

256. (Below) No. 2 shaft, Grimethorpe, finally filled. *Ian Walker*

257-259. The old colliery complex and industrial landscape at Grimethorpe, transformed beyond recognition by blasting and heavy plant clearance work during 1994. *Ian Walker*

260. The former Grimethorpe miner, Councillor Arthur Whittaker, served as Mayor of Barnsley 2000-2001. *Stan Plus Two*

261. Playright Stan Barstow, deputy head Mel Dyke and Barnsley MP Eric Illsley at Willowgarth High School, Grimethorpe, in front of a superb display of mining paintings. *Mel Dyke*

262. The Bishop of Wakefield, Nigel McCulloch, takes time to admire the artwork, under the guidance of Mel Dyke. *Mel Dyke*

263. Pictures of miners painted by Mark Britton were officially unveiled by the Mayor of Barnsley, Councillor Judith Watts and the Mayor of Brierley, Councillor Pat Doyle at the Willowgarth High School Presentation Night, Thursday 24 November 1994, when guest of honour was Rodney Bickestaffe, Associate General Secretary of the trade union UNISON. This is one of two tall portraits and is based on the face of Grimethorpe miner Johnny Wood. *Mel Dyke*

IN MEMORY OF
THOSE WHO HAVE LOST THEIR LIVES
IN SUPPORTING THEIR UNION
IN TIMES OF STRUGGLE

264. Standing outside the NUM premises in Barnsley is a superb bronze representation of a miner and his family. It was commissioned in 1993 by the Yorkshire Area NUM and is by well-known local sculptor Graham Ibberson. At the unveiling ceremony National President Arthur Scargill referred to the tragic deaths of three miners who were killed during recent disputes: Fred Matthews (1972), David Gareth Jones and Joe Green (both 1984/85). He also cited James Gibb and James Duggan, shot dead by the army at Featherstone during the 1893 lock-out. A full council chamber was reminded of the the dedicated work of the former miners' leader John Normansall who died, aged 45, from pneumonia contracted from repeatedly going underground after the terrible Swaithe Main disaster of December 1875 when 143 men and boys perished. *Brian Elliott*

Top: The Grimethorpe Pit site as it is today – being reclaimed. And above: Grimethorpe Colliery as it was. (BCPC)

Former pit sites give job hopes

By Ian Thompson

MORE THAN 1,000 jobs are expected to be created on the former pit sites at Grimethorpe and Park Springs at Houghton.

Mobile telecommunications, engineering and drugs companies from America, Asia and the Pacific as well as smaller local businesses are being targeted.

Colour brochures and other promotional literature is to be produced to market the sites to investors.

It will be paid for out of a grant of £270,711 from Europe which was awarded this week.

Over the next two years, some 75 hectares at Grimethorpe and 28 hectares at Houghton will be reclaimed so that factories and offices can be built.

Nigel Tipple, executive officer of the Grimethorpe Regeneration Executive, said: "We can offer large bits of land on both sites that would be suit mobile telecommunications, engineering and pharmaceutical companies wanting to move to the UK from Europe and further afield.

"We also hope to attract smaller, growing businesses set up by local people. It is a case of marketing both sites so companies know what the development opportunities are."

The efforts to market the Houghton and Grimethorpe sites was one of 14 projects to receive Euro-cash.

Greg Dyche, acting regional director of the Government Office for Yorkshire and the Humber, said:

"The money will help attract new investment and ensure that new and expanding employers in the region have access to a workforce will relevant skills."

● Part of a sum of £200,000 will be spent on marketing Elsecar, Cannon Hall, the Old Moor Wetlands at Broomhill and the Yorkshire Sculpture Park as major tourist attractions.

A further £249,000 will be spent on marketing the second phase of the Earth Centre at Denaby.

265. Regeneration at Grimethorpe and Houghton - with the help of money from Europe, as reported in the *Barnsley Chronicle*, 28 May 1999.

From coal face to fast food counter

By David Walsh

A FORMER Cortonwood miner is behind the opening of a McDonald's restaurant which has created 50 jobs.

The £1m investment has produced an 85-seat drive-thru which opens today – the fifth McDonald's in Barnsley.

Steve Taylor, 43, worked at the pit for 12 years until it closed in the 1980s, then – faced with unemployment – he took a counter job with the fast-food chain.

In 1998 he persuaded the property manager to have a look at Cortonwood after spotting its potential while the Dearne Towns Link Road was under construction.

He is still smiling about the bonus that visit eventually earned him.

"Its marvellous. I'm not nostalgic for the pit days, it is the way the world is going. Now I work in a suit, drive a new car and have a much better lifestyle."

As a miner, Steve, of Saltersbrook Road, Darfield, spent years working at 3ft high coal face for up to six hours a day.

Now he is an assistant manager responsible for audits and security systems at 54 restaurants including the new one – he will work there himself for a day a month.

"There is a tremendous difference, I started on the counter and even preferred that compared to the dust, heat and bad conditions and since then I've been promoted twice."

It will be opened at 11.30am today by Wentworth MP John Healey.

Restaurant manger Richard Glover said: "We have already had a positive response from the local community, and will be talking to representatives further to establish how we can get fully involved in local activities."

The regeneration of the site is virtually complete after development over the last three years which has created about 1,250 jobs.

It is now home to a Morrison's supermarket, a Post Office call centre, a handful of factories and a housing development. A giant Sainsbury's Homebase bringing 250 jobs is set to open at Easter.

Steve Taylor outside the new McDonald's at Cortonwood. (D

266. Regeneration at Brampton – the *Barnsley Chronicle* of 27 October 1999, reports the opening of a McDonald's fast food outlet ('the fifth in Barnsley') and the story of former Cortonwood miner, Steve Taylor.

267. The great Grimethorpe tradition of winning first aid prizes continues: a four-man team donned twenty-year old blue overalls, white shirts and white miners' belts in memory of the pit that closed and triumphed over 24 others at Buxton to become the St John Ambulance Grand Priors Championship of Champions in November 2000. They are (Left to Right): James Whitehead, Darren Whitehead, Glynn Sellars and Peter Connelly. For James it was the pinnacle of a lifetime in first aid, starting at the age of twelve. All four lads work for Hayley Bearings in South Kirkby. *Barnsley Chronicle*

UP to 100 jobs could be created in Grimethorpe next summer thanks to £1.5 million plans to build three factories.

The former pit site off Park Springs Road has been targeted for the scheme which has been drawn up by the Grimethorpe Regeneration Executive and development agency Yorkshire Forward.

An application for planning permission is expected to be submitted before Christmas and work could start in February, to be completed in early June.

Moving

Nigel Tipple, Grimethorpe Regeneration Executive chief executive, said: "We expect the factories to bring around 200 jobs to the village.

"The units may be occupied by companies moving in from outside or by firms already here which want to expand."

A grant to help build the three factories has ben secured from the European Regional Development Fund.

268. (Left) Plans to build three factories at the former pit site at Park Spring Road have been drawn up by Grimethorpe Regeneration and Yorkshire Forward, with the support of the European Regional Development Fund: *The Star*, 16 October 2000.

269. (Right) Waste 'pit concrete' is being recycled at Grimethorpe, according to this report in the *Barnsley Chronicle*, 27 October 2000.

By Sarah Wadsworth

WASTE concrete from the old Grimethorpe pit is being recycled to help build roads in the village.

Around 4,000 tonnes will be used for a 750-metre stretch of environmentally-friendly road.

The scheme is the first of its type in South Yorkshire and is part of plans to redevelop the Grimethorpe area.

Until now, the debris would have had to be ferried to landfill dumps but because it is being used on the site, there are financial as well as environmental benefits.

Geoff Birkett, Barnsley Council's assistant director of highways and engineering said: "We are continually looking for more energy-efficient, environmentally-friendly and cost-effective solutions for road building.

"The environmental advantages of the new technique are significant."

270. Actor Pete Postlethwaite returned to Grimethorpe in December 2000 to open the Millennium Green in the village where *Brassed Off* was filmed.

Pete is pictured here with cornet player Richard Marshall of Grimethorpe Colliery Band. He was presented with a coal sculpture created by former Grimethorpe Colliery miner Allan Armstrong. Perhaps, Pete's words, quoted in the *Barnsley Chronicle*, provide a fitting end to a century of life and events in Grimethorpe and Barnsley:

It's humbling to see the growth and changes that have occurred here.

All the Best!
Pete Postlethwaite.

A Barnsley Coalfield Chronology : 1900-2000

'This Government sees great future prospects for the mining industry'
Margaret Thatcher, House of Commons, June, 1984

1900   18 June:Yorkshire Miners' Association Demonstration in Barnsley; speakers include Barnsley MP Joseph Walton.
Minimum age for entering mining industry reduced to thirteen.

1901   22 January: death of Queen Victoria.

1902   Dearne Valley Colliery at Little Houghton in production.
Tankersley Colliery Rescue Station is built: first in Britain.
'Bag Muck Strike': mining families evicted from their homes at Denaby.

1903   16 December:death of Edward Cowey (64), President of the Yorkshire Miners' Association. He is succeeded by John Wadsworth.

1904   4 February: death of Benjamin Pickard, MP, first Secretary of the Yorkshire Miners' Association and President of the Miners' Federation of Great Britain from 1889, aged 61.
22 April: House of Commons approves a Bill which allows 'peaceful picketing' by trade unionists.
21 May:South Yorkshire Brass Band Association contest held in Barnsley.
20 June:Yorkshire Miners' Demonstration in Barnsley.

1905   Sinking of Elsecar Main.
3 October: evictions at Kinsley, near Hemsworth.

1906   Herbert Smith elected President of the Yorkshire Miners.

1907   11 April: great fire destroys surface buildings at Church Lane (Dodworth) Colliery.
16 November: seven men were killed in a terrible cage accident at Barrow Colliery.
23 November: four men killed in a boiler-house accident, Parkgate Seam, at Hoyland Silkstone Colliery, Platts Common.
17 June: Yorkshire Miners' Demonstration in Barnsley; speakers include Keir Hardie, MP for Merthyr Tydfil.

1908   *Eight Hours Act* for miners working underground resulted in considerable unrest in the northern coalfields where hewers were already working a six and seven hour day.
March: Francis Chandler presented with the Edward Medal ('miners' VC') in a ceremony at Buckingham Palace: awarded for his bravery in the explosion at the Hoyland Silkstone accident.

1909   Vernon Colliery, Worsbrough Common sunk.
Miners' union affiliates to the Labour Party.

1910   Miss Fountain cuts sod for new shafts at Woolley.
344 men and boys killed in an explosion at Hulton Colliery, Lancashire, Britain's second worst mining disaster (after Barnsley's Oaks Colliery disaster of 1866).
September-November: Home Secretary Winston Churchill orders troops into Rhonnda where, with fixed bayonets, they charged striking miners.
3 October: two men killed at Darfield Main.

1911   19 June:Yorkshire Miners' Demonstration in Barnsley: speakers include Keir Hardie.
11 July: three men killed at Grimethorpe Colliery when a steam valve burst.
Coal Mines Act.

1912   29 February: first national coalfield strike. Miners demand for a minimum wage of five shillings (25p) a day for men and two shillings (10p) for boys rejected by Prime Minister Asquith.
4 April: end of the 'great coal strike'.
24 April: Barnsley FC win the FA Cup in a reply at Bramall Lane, Sheffield.

7 July: three men killed in an explosion at Barnsley Main.

9 July: 87 miners and rescuers killed in explosions at Cadeby Colliery.

10 July: King George V visits Elsecar Main Colliery.

1913 1 April: Barnsley achieves 'County Borough' status, its population having exceeded 50,000 at the 1911 census.

UK coal production at its peak: 287 million tonnes (1.1 million men).

14 October: Senghenydd (S.Wales): 439 men and boys killed (UK's worst mining disaster).

1914 30 May: an explosion kills 11 men at Wharncliffe Silkstone Colliery, regarded as one of the safest pits in Yorkshire. At the start of the Great War about 500,000 men employed in the coal mining industry.

Barnsley regarded as the principal 'coal town' of Yorkshire.

11 August: Parkgate seam reached at Darton Main ('Jaggers') Colliery.

1915 Many Barnsley miners respond to Kitchener's call to arms and a Barnsley Battalion is launched.

1916 National shortage of coal.

1917 March: Government takes over control of mines.

1918 End of hostilities.

1919 23 January:150,000 miners join national strikes for a shorter working week.

11 February: Government offers miners a pay rise and sets up a royal commission (Sankey) to investigate the coal industry.

12 February: miners reject Government terms.

21 March: Government coal commission recommends a two shilling (10p) increase in pay for miners for a seven hour day.

21 July: coal strike in Yorkshire.

25 July: four-day coal strike settled as miners accept a 14.2 per cent increase in piece rates.

24 November: Government announces a ten shillings (50p) per ton cut in the price of coal.

Skiers Spring Colliery (Newton Chambers) under development.

Primrose Colliery, Smithies, re-opened.

1920 16 October: national coal miners' strike begins.

3 November: miners' strike called off despite a small voting majority in favour of continuance.

Mining Industry Act: output levy enabled 'welfare provision', money that would be used for pit-head baths, canteens etc.

Coal production in Britain reaches 229 million tonnes.

1921 3 March: *Unemployment Act,* benefit increased to £1 per week for men and 18 shillings (63p) for women. There are c.1 million people registered unemployed.

31 March: mines returned to private ownership. Coal owners propose a 50 per cent cut in miners' pay.

1 April: miners' union refused to agree to such a drastic wage cut: owners lock miners out of pits and government declares a 'state of emergency', drafting troops into the coalfields.

3 April: coal rationing.

15 April: 'Black Friday', railway and transport unions withdraw support of Miners' Federation dispute, leaving miners alone in their dispute with coal owners.

16 June: pit pony races held at Darfield in aid of miners' distress fund.

28 June: coal strike ends, government agrees to subsidize the coal industry but miners are c20 per cent worse off in real terms (cf 1914).

4 July: miners return to work.

31 July: 'Red Friday', Baldwin government provide state subsidy of £24 million to offset wage cuts of miners.

1922   Herbert Smith, Yorkshire miners' leader is elected as National President of the union.
         October: Arthur Hatcher is awarded Edward Medal for his bravery in saving the lives of
         four men by stopping a runaway tub at Barnsley Main.
         15 November: Conservatives (Bonar Law et al) win general election.
1923   1,297 men killed and 212,256 men injured: 'Marshall a procession, four men in a
         rank, one and a half yards apart, forty-five miles long with every fifteen yards an
         ambulance to hospital, every sixty-one yards a hearse' (Yorkshire miners' leader,
         Herbert Smith). For the next ten years more than a thousand men and boys were – on
         average – killed every year.
         6 December: General Election results in a Labour victory.
1924   22 January: First Labour government under Ramsey McDonald.
         A.J. Cooke elected as Secretary of Miners' Federation (of GB).
         Joseph Jones becomes General Secretary of the Yorkshire Miners.
         29 October: Conservatives win general election; Baldwin to begin second term of office as PM.
1925   19 August: miners agree to take part in the government's enquiry into their pay.
         Coal owners withdraw their demands for longer working hours and lower wages in lieu
         of Treasury subsidizing further losses,ending a month-long crisis in the coal industry.
         Royal Commission (under Sir Herbert Samuel)set up to examine the state of coal
         industry.
1926   24 March: Government accepts report of coal commission.
         Miners' leader, A.J. Cook's response: 'Not a penny off the pay, not a minute on the day'.
         Miners' Federation of Great Britain refuses to accept recommendation of Royal
         Commission that wages must be cut.
         30 April: national coal stoppage in response to owners' demand to return to their 1921
         minimum wage structure. Miners appeal to whole of trade union movement for support.
         1 May: state subsidy to miners ends;miners go on strike.
         4 May: General Strike. Troops deployed in Yorkshire.
         12 May: TUC calls off general strike leaving miners alone and bitter over 'desertion'.
         Coal picking at many locations.
         18 August: miners reopen negotiations with government.
         Soup kitchens and great distress in Barnsley, Hoyle Mill, Hoyland Common and many
         other places. Jump Distress Committee 'feeds a thousand daily'.
         5 October: 250,000 striking miners have returned to work.
         12 November: agreement reached to end the six month pit strike:working hours to be
         increased from seven to eight, and future agreements to be negotiated locally not
         nationally. However, the dispute continued for months more in some areas, with utter
         destitution.
1927   28 June: *Trade Dispute Act* declares 'sympathetic' strikes as illegal.
         23 November: Prime Minister Baldwin refuses to meet 200 Welsh miners who had
         walked 180 miles from the Rhondda to London.
         A.J.Cook warns PM of 'a revolutionary situation' developing due to unemployment and
         distress in the mining industry.
         Vernon Colliery, Worsbrough Common, closed.
1929   The Prince of Wales expresses sympathy to mining communities due to their low wages
         and poor housing conditions when touring the north of England.
         30 May: general election win for Labour and Second Ramsey McDonald government.
1931   27 July: UK unemployment reaches a record 2.7 million.
         20 November: an explosion at Bentley Colliery, near Doncaster results in the death of
         42 miners.
         Means Test introduced for long-term unemployed.
         All party National Government under McDonald's leadership (to 1935).

1932   Woolley Colliery 'completely electrified'.
       Mottram Wood colliery abandoned.
       20 June: Yorkshire Miners' Association Demonstration in Barnsley (the first since
       1911): speakers include MP's George Landsbury and Herbert Morrison.
       10 October: Barnsley Mining and Technical College opens.
1933   19 June: Yorkshire Miners' Demonstration in Barnsley: speakers include Ernest Bevin.
1934   262 men killed in the Gresford pit disaster, near Wrexham.
1935   19 miners killed in an explosion at North Gawber Colliery.
       Average miners' wage £114 per annum.
       56,000 Yorkshire miners out of work.
1936   11 March: George Orwell arrives in Barnsley to collect material for a new book. He
       stays in the house of miner Albert Gray, 4 Agnes Terrace.
       15 March: Oswald Mosley speaks at the Harvey Institute, Barnsley.
       19 March: Orwell goes down a 'day hole' pit (the Wentworth) and two days later down
       Grimethorpe Colliery.
       22 June: Yorkshire Miners' Demonstration in Barnsley: speakers include Clement
       Attlee, Leader of the Labour Party.
       6 August: 57 miners killed at Old Carlton pit (Wharncliffe Woodmoor 1, 2 and 3).
       The Coal Scuttle by Joseph Jones (Mayor of Barnsley and President of Miners' Federation
       of Great Britain) published.
       5 October: the 'Jarrow Crusade' of jobless begin long march to London, miners
       prominent. Activists include Arthur Horner and Will Paynter (who were to become
       miners' union leaders) and miners' agent Nye Bevan.

1937   9 March: publication of Orwell's *The Road to Wigan Pier*.
       21 June: Yorkshire Miners' Demonstration in Barnsley.
       October: King George VI and Queen Elizabeth visit Barnsley Mining and Technical
       College.
1938   Herbert Smith, most respected miners' leader of the 1920s and 1930s dies at his office
       desk in Barnsley.
       Joseph Jones resigns as General Secretary of the Yorkshire Miners to take up a post with
       the new Coal Commission whose remit included pit 'amalgamations' in order to
       concentrate production at 'economic pits'.
       Joseph Hall, a brilliant speaker and exponent of miners' rights and social justice is new
       President of the Yorkshire miners.
1939   Pit-head baths opened at Woolley and North Gawber collieries.
       How Green was My Valley published by Richard Llewellyn.
       Outbreak of Second World War.
1940   Pit-head baths opened at Wombwell Main.
       6 May: UK unemployment now below 1m.
1942   New canteen opens at Dearne Valley Colliery.
1943   2 December: 'Bevin Boys' (1 in 10 of young conscripts) are called up to work down the
       mines.
1945   1 January: formation of National Union of Mineworkers.
       Labour Party landslide election victory.
1946   22 January: pit owners protest at Labour's plans to nationalize coal mines.
       24 July: Fuel Minister Emanuel Shinwell warns of coal stocks being exhausted during
       the winter.
       Coal Mines Nationalization Act creates the National Coal Board.
1947   1 January: 'Vesting Day': nationalization of the coal industry. The new National Coal
       Board responsible for c.1,500 mines employing c.692,000 men.

February: One of worst winters ever known at a time when fuel was in very short supply.
21 June: Yorkshire Miners' Demonstration in Barnsley: speakers include Prime
Minister Attlee and Minister of Fuel and Power Shinwell.
Nine men killed in an explosion at Barnsley Main Colliery.
'Stint strike' at Grimethorpe spreads to other collieries, Miners and
government agree 5 day week.

1948   31 January: New National Coal Board lost £5.44 million in last quarter of 1947.
13 July: The NCB lost over £23million in the first year of nationalization 608 miners
were killed and 2,447 seriously injured.
Darton Main ('Jaggers') closes.

1949   December: A carol service is held underground at Redbrook pit, becoming an annual
event until the early 1960s.

1950   80 miners killed in an underground fire at Cresswell, Derbyshire.
Miners head 'industrial wages league' for first time.

1951   February: Winter fuel shortage.
Pit-head baths opened at Dearne Valley Colliery.

1952   Joe Hall, who was born at Lundhill in 1887 and at the age of twelve started work at
Darfield Main, retires as President of the Yorkshire Miners. He is succeeded by Alwin
Machin.
Pit-head baths opened at Barnsley Main.
14 June: Yorkshire Miners' Demonstration in Barnsley: speakers include Herbert
Morrison MP.

1953   31 March: Roy Mason, a former Carlton miner, aged 29, becomes Barnsley's youngest
ever MP.

1954   130 Yorkshire pits employ c.150,000 men.

1955   National Day-Wage Agreement.

1956   Mitchell's Main (Wombwell) closes.

1957   Woolley Colliery employs 2,390 workers.

1958   June: Yorkshire Miners' Demonstration in Barnsley also celebrates the centenary of the
South Yorkshire Miners' Association: Harold Wilson, MP, is one of speakers.
July: Yorkshire Area NUM Summer School at Bingley.

1959   Ventilation shaft sunk at Woolley.
20 June: Yorkshire Miners' Demonstration in Barnsley: Barbara Castle MP and W.E.
Jones, President of NUM are main speakers.

1960   Alwin Machin, Yorkshire miners' leader and responsible for so many educational
innovations for miners, is elected National President but dies on the day the result is
announced.
Sam Bullough succeeds Machin as President of the Yorkshire miners.

1961   January: Silkstone Common pit closes and merged with Wentworth Silkstone.
Lord Robens is new Chairman of the NCB.

1965   19 June: Yorkshire Miners' Gala in Barnsley: speakers include George Brown MP (First
Secretary of State) and Lord Collinson (Chairman of TUC).

1966   National Power Loading Agreement.
May: Barnsley Main closes (745 jobs).
August: Wharncliffe Woodmoor 1,2 and 3 (Old Carlton) closes (847 men employed).
Major discoveries of oil and gas in North Sea.
27 October: Coal tip buries a Welsh school at Aberfan killing 116 children.
December: Monckton collieries (1, 2, 6 and 3,4) close (2,273 men employed).

1967   Wharncliffe Silkstone (Tankersley) closes and merges with Rockingham.
A motion by the Woolley branch over pit closures against Roy Mason, the Barnsley
NUM – sponsored MP and Labour's new Minister of Fuel and Power is defeated by 96

votes to 8 in the Yorkshire Miners' Council.

Elsecar Main produces a million tons in a year.

1968   April: Monk Bretton Colliery closes (889 men employed).

1969   May: Wombwell Main closes (670 men employed).

Woolley produces 1 million tonnes with a reduced workforce of 1,931.

21 June: Yorkshire Miners' Gala in Barnsley: speakers include Roy Mason MP and Lawrence Daly (Secretary, NUM).

The militant left in the NUM 'in the ascendancy'.

10-24 October: unofficial strikes in support of pay for surface workers ends with Lord Robens agreeing to a wage claim (£1.7s.6d per week) in full.

Alan Plater's Close the Coal House Door.

1970   July: Wharncliffe Woodmoor 4 & 5 pit (Carlton Main)closes (860 men employed).

Ken Loache's film *Kes* (based on Barry Hine's book A Kestral for a Knave, filmed in Barnsley, has its 'Yorkshire premier' at the *Ritz* cinema.

Majority for strike action changed from two-thirds to 55 per cent by NUM Conference in Scotland.

October: unofficial strikes break out.

1971   Joe Gormley defeats Mick McGahey to become NUM president.

Since appointment of Lord Robens c.400 pits have closed and 300,000 jobs lost in the coal mining industry.

1 November: NCB refuse to negotiate with miners re demands for better pay: a national overtime ban imposed.

1972   Skiers Spring pit closes.

8/9 January: national miners' strike: the first since 1926. All 289 pits out.

20 January: UK unemployment now over 1 million.

3 February: Fred Matthews, a Hatfield miner, is killed whilst secondary picketing at Keadby power station.

10 February: engineers, transport workers and other unions go on strike.

16 February: electricity blackouts and three-day working week. 'Victory for Miners' pickets' at Saltley coke depot, Birmingham.

18 February: Wilberforce Enquiry recommends a £6 pw pay increase to miners.

25 February: miners accept pay offer by 27:1 majority: £34.50 for face workers,£25 for other underground workers and £23 for surface workers.

Government incomes policy breached by miners.

1973   Ferrymoor pit closes and merges with Riddings.

Seven miners killed at Lofthouse Colliery, near Wakefield.

Now only 78 pits in Yorkshire (52 having been closed since 1953).

9 August: petrol rationing coupons printed due to oil crisis.

13 November: miners and power workers take industrial action: Heath government declares 'state of emergency'.

17 December: miners' overtime ban continues. Industry and commerce to be restricted to three days electricity.

Arthur Scargill succeeds Sam Bullough as President of National Union of Mineworkers' Yorkshire Area and Owen Briscoe is new General Secretary.

1974   4 February: miners ballot: 81 per cent in favour of a national strike.

7 February: Tory PM Heath announces a general election date of 28 February on 'Who rules Britain'.

6 March: Labour's Harold Wilson is new PM. Miners call off strike, and receive 35 per cent (£6-£15) pay increase.

8 March: five-day week resumes.

1 April: John Keirs is new Director of Barnsley Coalfield.

11 October: Labour win second general election in a year but by only three seats.

7 November: Yorkshire NUM celebrates the centenary of the official opening of the miners' offices in Barnsley.

Government's *A Plan For Coal* published.

National strike.

1975 11 February: Margaret Thatcher is new Tory leader.

13 February: UK miners accept pay award averaging 35 per cent.

12 June: five miners killed in an underground explosion at Houghton Main.

11 July: pay rises to be limited by law due to runaway inflation.

21 August: unemployment reaches 1.25 million.

21 June 1975: Yorkshire Miners' Gala in Barnsley: speakers include Michael Foot MP (Secretary of State for Employment) and Mick McGahey (Vice-President, NUM).

1976 1 April: Government announces plans to sink the world's largest pit near Selby.

Royston Drift Mine opens.

5 April: James Callaghan is new PM following Harold Wilson's resignation.

21,000 men in Barnsley Borough employed in coal mining (47 per cent of workforce).

Bower's Row by Jim Bullock published.

10 September: Barnsley MP Roy Mason appointed new Ulster Secretary.

1977 15 April: miners demand an end to the 'social contract' amid growing industrial unrest.

2 July: miners pay demand is for £135 and a four-day week, but a plea for moderation from NUM president Joe Gormley.

1978 Incentive Scheme introduced.

July: Wentworth Silkstone (Stainborough) closes (250 men employed).

Seven miners killed at Bentley Colliery, near Doncaster.

1979 31 January: 'Winter of discontent': rubbish piles up amid industrial chaos.

4 May: new PM Margaret Thatcher celebrates Tory election win.

16 June: Yorkshire Miners' Gala in Barnsley: speakers include Clive Jenkins (Secretary, ASTMS) and labour MP Tony Benn.

13 November: miners reject a 20 per cent pay increase and threaten industrial action in pursuit of a 65 per cent claim.

November: Rockingham Colliery (at Hoyland) closes (252 men employed).

1980 22 July: UK unemployment (1.9 million) is worst since 1930s.

Kellingley Colliery is first pit to produce 2 million tonnes in a year.

1981 14,834 miners employed in Barnsley area coalfield.

September: Arthur Scargill publishes pamphlet *Miners in the Eighties* and is elected as President of the NUM by a record majority (70.3 per cent).

1982 Autumn. Arthur Scargill announces at a press conference that a 'secret NCB document', prepared by the Monopolies and Mergers Commission, shows that 75-95 pits will close over ten years.

1983 1 September: former British Steel chief Ian MacGregor starts work as Chairman of NCB.

18 June: Yorkshire Miners' Gala in Barnsley: speakers include John Mortimer (Secretary of Labour Party) and Peter Heathfield (Secretary, Derbyshire NUM).

Peoples March for Jobs.

October: Elsecar Main closes (300 men employed).

1 November: NUM start overtime ban.

1984 1 March: NCB announces plans to close 20 pits (c.20,000 jobs),including Cortonwood.

8/9 March: NUM executive grants permission for areas to strike in defence of pits and jobs. A young Yorkshire miner, David Jones is killed on a picket line at Ollerton, Notts.

19 April: Special Delegate Conference held in Sheffield calls on all areas and members to strike.

Many Nottinghamshire miners refuse to support the strike call,arguing for a national ballot.

12 May: 'Women's Day of Action' in Barnsley.

Picketing so effective that a massive co-ordinated police operation is established. The dispute becomes the most bitter in trade union history.

May-July: at Orgreave Coking Plant police use riot gear, horses, dogs and vehicles against miners.

15 June: Yorkshire miner Joe Green crushed to death on picket duty at Ferrybridge.

October-November: NUM funds sequestrated and union placed in hands of a receiver.

Christmas celebrated at 'The Alamo' (Cortonwood) and other picket outposts.

1985   2 March: Yorkshire Area votes to continue strike.

3 March: NUM Special Conference voted to end the strike by a very small majority (3 votes) and return to work without negotiating with the NCB.

5 March: national strike officially ends after 12 months.

Barrow and Dodworth pits close. 1,200 men transfer from Barrow to Barnsley Main. Barnsley Main re-opens and there is a 'new pit' at Redbrook.

Grimethorpe, administrative offices of Barnsley Coalfield closes and the Barnsley Area Coalfield merges with North Yorkshire Area.

6 July: Nottinghamshire miners break from the NUM and form Union of Democratic Mineworkers.

179,000 UK miners now employed in 133 collieries.

25 October: Cortonwood Colliery closes (690 men employed).

Elsecar Colliery buildings demolished.

December: North Gawber colliery closes (merged with Woolley).

1986   14 March: Miners at Grimethorpe Colliery achieve their highest-ever tonnage for a single coal face (17,338 tonnes in a week, from Newhill seam).

13 December: A £2m scheme to open a Yorkshire Mining Museum is launched at Caphouse Colliery near Wakefield.

NUM move into new headquarters in Sheffield: Cambridge House, Barker's Pool.

Ian Macgregor Knighted.

1987   20 June: Yorkshire Miners' (one hundredth) Gala and Demonstration in Barnsley: speakers include Neil Kinnock (Leader of Labour party) and Arthur Scargill, (NUM President).

Redbrook Colliery closes.

Woolley Colliery closes.

Publication of *Pits* by John Threlkeld: *A Pictorial Record of Mining in Barnsley*.

Houghton/Darfield produces 'the fastest million tonnes in the Barnsley coalfield', previously (1981) held by Grimethorpe.

1988   Ferrymoor/Riddings and Redbrook close.

Shafts at Cortonwood capped.

Grimethorpe produces a record 5 tonnes per man shift.

1989   Darfield Main and Royston Drift Mine close.

British Coal announce doubling of profits to almost £500 million from a workforce now of less than 100,000.

A Century of Struggle, British Miners in Pictures published by the NUM in celebration of the 100th anniversary of the formation of the National Miners' Union.

NUM/MFGB gala in Barnsley.

John Threlkeld's *Pits 2* published.

1991   Barnsley Main closes.

Dearne Valley closes

1992   Only 59 pits in Yorkshire: just 2 pits remain open in the old Barnsley coalfield: Grimethorpe and Houghton Main.

13 October: Michael Heseltine, President of the Board of Trade, announces that 31 pits (including Grimethorpe and Houghton) are to cease production with a loss of 30,000 jobs, almost a third of them in Yorkshire. Board of Trade President announces a £1bn redundancy package and 'help' for mining areas. Just 19 pits to remain open nationwide.

14 October: Coal Minister Tim Eggar tells councillors who came to see him for help to regenerate their areas that they must deal with redundancies 'locally'. Some help.
'Life After Coal' campaign launched by *Yorkshire Post*.
Sponsorship of brass bands withdrawn.

15 October: the pit closure announcement 'lacked cabinet approval'

16 October: Willowgarth High School, Grimethorpe and Yorkshire Arts Circus announce plans to produce a book 'before the colliery closes.'

21 October: Labour motion calling for no pit closures defeated by 320 votes to 307 after government make 'further concessions'. 21 (of the 31) pits to be placed under 'a review process'. John Major is described as 'the most unpopular Premier in polling history' by Mori. 'Coal Not Dole': thousands of miners pour into London in 'a crusade for coal'.

30 October: Houghton Main and Grimethorpe close.

November: 'Save Our Pits' rally in Barnsley town centre.
Petition handed in to 10 Downing Street by nine year old Michael Sykes of Grimethorpe.

1993   2 February: Two pupils from Willowgarth High School (Claire Greeson and Sally Middleton) Grimethorpe travel to London to present to 10 Downing Street a book celebrating the life of their community: *Energy is Coal - The Grimethorpe Pit Closure.*
25 March: Government's White Paper *The Prospects for Coal* published: a stay of execution only where British Coal 'reduces costs' and 'finds new markets' prior to full privatization of the industry. Decisions on pit closures are 'for British Coal'. In other words the closure plan continues.
30 April: Houghton Main closes.
7 May: Grimethorpe Colliery closes.
22 October: British Coal decide to demolish historic pit buildings at Grimethorpe and Houghton Main despite mounting protests from individuals, Barnsley councillors and members of the Coalfields' Communities Campaign.
3 December: Work starts on reclaiming Barnsley Main colliery yard, the main headgear buildings and track to be kept as 'historic features'.

1994   4 February: Goldthorpe Main Colliery closes.
British Coal starts selling off its sites.
1 April: Coalite Smokeless Fuels announce closure of its plant at Grimethorpe.
15 July: NUM 'merges' with Yorkshire and the interior of the old Yorkshire miners' compensation department offices at Huddersfield Road, Barnsley – on an upper floor – is refurbished to accommodate Arthur Scargill.

1995   Royal Commission of Historic Monuments (at request of English Heritage) begins emergency programme of recording pit sites by aerial photography.

1996   The film *Brassed Off* receives critical praise.
15 June: (last?)Yorkshire Miners' Gala and Demonstration held in Barnsley.
Route of march from Churchfield to Civic Hall (Eldon Street). Speakers include Ken Livingstone MP.

1997   December. British Coal dissolved, remaining liabilities transferred to DTI.

1998   Only 12 collieries in operation in Yorkshire, all but one (Hatfield) owned by RJB Mining.
October: Oaks Colliery 'angel statue' returned to its plinth on Doncaster Road,

	Kendray Hill, following restoration and numerous attempts to damage and steal the historic monument.
1999	New Morrison's supermarket on part of old Cortonwood site.
	Barnsley is chosen as one of 22 towns to be a 'pit disease test centre'.
	30 December: old colliery sites 'to play a vital part in new Barnsley' with development companies planning to use them as business parks.
2000	Factory units and and new housing planned for former Cortonwood area of Brampton by St Paul's Developments.
	28 May: over 1,000 jobs expected to be created on the former pit sites at Grimethorpe and Park Springs (Houghton), according to Grimethorpe Regeneration Executive.
	6 October: work is due to start on a £2.4m enterprise park on the former Wharncliffe Woodmoor 1, 2 and 3 site at Carlton, via grants from Yorkshire Forward and English Partnerships.
	16 October: the former Grimethorpe pit site could be used for a £1.5m scheme to build three factories (Grimethorpe Regeneration Executive).
	27 October: McDonald's open an 85 seat and 'drive thru' restaurant at Brampton where Cortonwood pit once stood.
	Former 'pit concrete' from the old Grimethorpe pit is being recycled to build roads in the village.
	Billy Elliot, set during the 1984/85 strike, is 'the best British film' of the year.
	21 December: actor Pete Postlethwaite helps celebrate new regeneration monument at Millennium Green, Grimethorpe.

Former Grimethorpe miner Allan Armstrong (b.1923) has many artistic talents. Here he can be seen displaying a copy of his autobiography and a specially commissioned coal sculpture *Brassed Off* which was presented to actor Pete Postlethwaite in December 2000. Behind him, a small selection of mining scenes. *Barnsley Chronicle*